AMERICAN COOKERY

About the Author

Lynette Baxter gained a degree in Home Economics from the University of Surrey, which led to a career in the food industry. She works on product and recipe development for major high street retailers, with a particular interest in introducing exciting new flavours from around the world. She has a firm belief that anyone can cook anything armed with a good recipe and hopes that this book will encourage others to feel the same.

★★ SPECIALITY KITCHEN ★★

THE BEST OF

AMERICAN COOKERY

Lynette Baxter

BLITZ EDITIONS

Acknowledgements

Design: Amanda Hawkes
Illustrations: Lesley Cullen
Cover photograph: Jhon Kevern
Editor: Nicola Baxter

The author and publishers wish to thank
Myrus Youngs and Adrian Reeve
for their help with this book.

This edition first published by Blitz Editions
an imprint of Bookmart Limited
Registered Number 2372865
Trading as Bookmart Limited, Desford Road, Enderby,
Leicester, LE9 5AD, England

Produced for Bookmart Limited by Nicola Baxter

Printed in Great Britain

CONTENTS

INTRODUCING AMERICAN COOKERY

As everybody knows, America is a big country. Its landscape and climate vary from the picturesque New England coast in the east to the sunshine of California in the west, from the steamy southern states to the rich pastures of the north. In the tropical temperatures of Florida, oranges can be picked from the trees. In an icy Wisconsin winter, the great outdoors is a much less attractive prospect. To demonstrate the enormous diversity of the USA, we have only to compare the two outlying states – Hawaii and Alaska!

Life in America is just as varied. The slick sophistication of its great cities seems a world away from the apparently timeless lifestyle of the countryside and small towns.

Yet perhaps America's greatest and richest diversity comes from its people. The population brings together cultures and customs from all over the globe. Every one of them has left its mark on what we think of as American cuisine. To the culinary skills of the indigenous Americans have been added influences from the early Spanish, English, Dutch and French explorers. The unhappy history of the slave trade brought a large African American population with its own styles of cooking. Scots, Irish, German, Scandinavian, Mexican and Asian immigrants have added their ingredients and methods too. Over the years, these populations have adapted their cuisines to the circumstances of life in America and there has been considerable sharing of traditions and techniques.

But what is American cookery? It is much harder to define than classic Indian or French cuisine, as each "classic" recipe has regional variations. The apple pie eaten in North Dakota may be barely recognisable as the dish of the same name in Louisiana. It is impossible here to do more than offer an appetiser to the glorious flavours of this cuisine. By including dishes from all over the country, I hope to introduce something of the diversity of regional dishes and tempt you to develop your own variations. Nothing could be more in keeping with the essence of American cookery.

Any discussion of the ethnic variety of American food must recognise that a flourishing range of foodstuffs was already well established before Europeans set foot on the American continent. The native Americans practised baking, stewing, barbecuing and steaming. They milled corn for their bread, preserved fish and meat by smoking, and used honey and maple syrup for sweetening. It is these people whom the first European settlers had to thank for their survival. Although they arrived with crops to plant, these proved quite unsuitable for the harsh winters of New England. It was the native Americans, teaching the skills of raising corn and beans and catching fish, who saved the newcomers from starvation.

As the various settlers and immigrants arrived and found their places in the vast land of America, so cuisines adapted to the conditions of each region. For example, the cooking of New England combines dishes that make the most of the sea's abundance, hearty stews and pot roasts to keep out the winter cold, and native American dishes such as cornbread. In Pennsylvania, Virginia and North Carolina, where the Dutch settled, pancakes, waffles and "cookies" were added to the culinary melting pot. African cooking traditions played an important role in the development of cooking in the southern states. Okra in soups and gumbos, and black-eyed peas and spices in many dishes are all thanks to this African influence. Oranges were introduced by the Spanish, the warm climate of Florida being ideal for their cultivation. In fact, both Spanish and French contributions can be seen throughout American cookery, such as in the increasingly popular Creole style.

As new waves of settlers and prospectors flooded west, recipes such as meatballs, fried chicken and hamburgers entered the cuisine, while "cowboy" cooking, barbecues and baked beans also proved ideal for a population on the move or hard at work.

Today's all-too-common perception of American food as mainly hamburgers and hot dogs ignores a vast history in which flavours have mingled and merged. Modern America seems to move at an ever faster pace in all aspects of life, including food. It may seem as though Americans never have time to cook properly and that the only food preparation they do is to press the buttons of their microwave ovens, but there is still a great tradition of cooking and several occasions throughout the year when food is particularly important. Fourth of July picnics and Thanksgiving dinners come immediately to mind.

An appreciation of good food and quality ingredients means that Americans frequently eat outside the home. Great steak houses, Italian restaurants and family diners all provide excellent meals for reasonable prices. A new pride in regional American specialities has grown in recent years, together with a new generation of chefs who are eager to cook traditional dishes.

Shops and Supermarkets

No one entering an American supermarket could doubt the nation's interest in food. An enormous range of products is available. The aisles of frozen pre-prepared foods are indeed extensive, but this is no longer all that is on offer. Three features of these stores in particular can scarcely be ignored.

Firstly, there is an enormous range and quality of fresh fruits and vegetables on display. In a medium-sized store in an average-sized town, I was amazed to see 19 varieties of eating apples, beautifully

polished and presented. Many delicate fruits and vegetables are arranged on beds of ice to retain their freshness, along with prepared fruit, such as peeled and sliced fresh pineapples and quartered and seeded melons. Prepared salads, both vegetable and fruit, are displayed in enormous and attractive variety.

Secondly, freezer cabinets contain a marvellous variety of ice creams and sorbets. These range from wickedly rich concoctions, based on cream and full of chocolate chips and fudge pieces, to deliciously light yoghurt-based ices, flavoured with fresh fruit.

Even more noticeable, however, on first entering the shop, is the enticing smell of the in-store bakery. A vast range of doughnuts – rings, fingers, rounds, plain or iced, with jam or custard fillings – are matched by the display of Danish pastries, muffins and cookies. Freshly baked pies – lemon meringue, key lime, Mississippi mud, pumpkin, apple and peach – will weaken even the most dedicated dieter's resolve. I make no apology for the fact that a large proportion of this book is devoted to baking and desserts – areas researched all-too-intensively on my travels in America! Baking is one of the cookery skills at which Americans excel. Many traditional recipes have survived, sometimes interestingly updated. Although healthy eating has influenced many areas of the American diet, home baking has remained – it's simply too good to give up!

In some respects, the vastness of America and its culinary variety presents its own problems. To transport food produced in the north of America to states like California involves a 3,000-mile trip, involving three or four days' driving. Husband and wife teams, one partner driving while the other sleeps, run huge trucks along the "interstates" all over America, making long-distance deliveries. This does help to explain why America buys so much of its food frozen. It is simply not possible to transport it any other way.

In recent years American influence on the cuisines of many countries has accelerated. Most obvious, perhaps, is the rise of fast-food restaurants. No high street is complete without at least one burger bar and fried chicken outlet. Sodas and colas have become popular drinks everywhere, while snacks such as peanuts and popcorn have also taken the journey across the Atlantic.

A wander around your local supermarket will show this influence. Shelves full of breakfast cereals, peanut butter (also available with "jelly" mixed in), pumpkins and squashes, deep-dish pizzas, muffins and bagels, cans of sweetcorn and ready made chilli con carne all bear witness to their American roots.

These days "traditional" pub food often consists of barbecued ribs, chilli, pizzas, hot wings, burgers, fried chicken and, of course, fries with everything! Quite frequently these will be washed down with American beers and soft drinks or even wine from California.

Today traditional American foods and ingredients are readily available, enabling us to enjoy these treats without extensive travel. American-style crisps, peanuts, tortillas and tacos, barbecue and chilli sauces, and hickory chips are just a few of the products that make it easy to cook American favourites. I hope that the recipes in this book will inspire you to try these for yourself.

Using These Recipes

You may have seen American cookery books and been confused by recipes giving measurements in cups. This book, although full of favourite American recipes, uses metric and imperial measures.

Conversion Tables

Remember...

Use metric or imperial measures, do not mix both within a recipe.

Spoon measures are level, unless otherwise specified.

The recipes in this book are based on size 3 eggs, but size 2 or 4 will be fine.

Where a recipe mentions a pinch of flavouring, it is literally the amount you can pick up between thumb and forefinger.

Weights

1/2 oz	10g	7oz	200g
1oz	25g	8oz	225g
1 1/2 oz	40g	9oz	250g
2oz	50g	10oz	275g
2 1/2 oz	60g	11oz	300g
3oz	75g	12oz	350g
3 1/2 oz	90g	14oz	400g
4oz	110g	1lb	450g
4 1/2 oz	125g	1 1/2 lb	700g
5oz	150g	2lb	900g
6oz	175g	3lb	1.5kg (1500g)

Measurements

1/8 inch	3mm	1 1/2 inches	4cm
1/4 inch	5mm	2 inches	5cm
1/2 inch	1cm	3 inches	7.5cm
3/4 inch	2cm	4 inches	10cm
1 inch	2.5cm	12 inches	30cm
1 1/4 inches	3cm		

Liquid Measures

5 fl oz	1/4 pt	150ml	15 fl oz	3/4 pt	425ml
7.5 fl oz		215ml	20 fl oz	1pt	570ml
10 fl oz	1/2 pt	275ml	35 fl oz	1 3/4pt	1 litre

Spoon Measures

1/2 tspn	2.5ml	2tbspn	30ml
1tspn	5ml	3tbspn	45ml
1 1/2 tspn	7.5ml	4tbspn	60ml
2tspn	10ml	5tbspn	75ml
1tbspn	15ml		

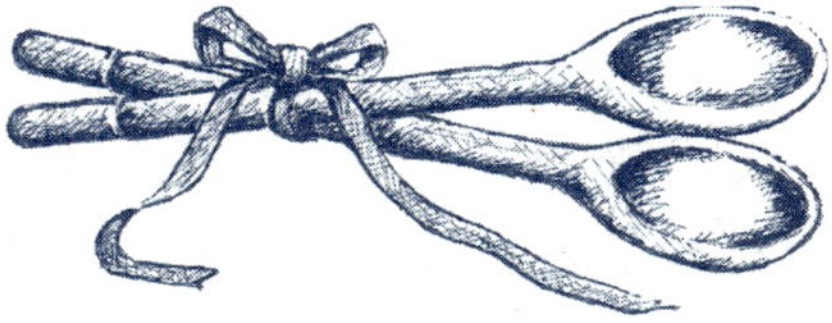

Oven Temperatures

Gas Mark 1	275°F	140°C	Gas Mark 5	375°F	190°C
Gas Mark 2	300°F	150°C	Gas Mark 6	400°F	200°C
Gas Mark 3	325°F	170°C	Gas Mark 7	425°F	220°C
Gas Mark 4	350°F	180°C	Gas Mark 8	450°F	230°C

Abbreviations

cm	centimetre	mm	millimetre
fl oz	fluid ounce	oz	ounce
g	gram	pt	pint
kg	kilogram	tbspn	tablespoon
ml	millilitre	tspn	teaspoon

Cup Measurements

An American cup holds 8 fluid ounces. This list shows some common ingredients with their metric and imperial equivalents.

1 cup granulated/caster sugar	225g	8oz
1 cup soft brown sugar	175g	6oz
1 cup oil	225g	8oz
1 cup butter	225g	8oz
1 cup grated cheese	90g	3½oz
1 cup walnuts	150g	5oz
1 cup cornmeal	150g	5oz
1 cup long grain rice	225g	8oz

If you have a cookbook with measurements in cups, all you need do is to find a large cup or small mug that holds between 7½ and 8½ fluid ounces of water. Cup measurements cannot be entirely accurate, so this will be close enough.

Equipment

You will find that you require very little additional equipment to make the recipes in this book. However, the following are "gadgets" that you might wish to acquire if you decide to become a dedicated American cook.

Waffle iron

The most basic of these are simply hinged moulds that can be heated on the hob. These are perfectly adequate but quite messy to use. You may prefer an electric model. I have a small electric grill that can have its cooking plates changed to turn it into a waffle maker or sandwich toaster.

Barbecues

In America barbecues have become so popular that there is now concern over potential smoke pollution and the public are being encouraged to use gas-fired barbecues. Perhaps gas barbecues do not give such a good flavour but they are certainly very convenient, if rather expensive. It is still possible to buy charcoal-fired barbecues very cheaply and there is all the fun of lighting them!

Griddles

Some might consider these necessary for sizzling steaks and frying pancakes. I have always found that a large, heavy based frying pan is perfectly adequate.

Muffin tins

True, muffin tins will produce the authentic article, but a slightly more modest cake, cooked in paper cases in bun tins, will taste every bit as good.

Microwave ovens

No, not to heat up your frozen meal, but for dozens of time-saving operations. Melting chocolate, dissolving gelatine and softening butter immediately spring to mind. If you do not already have a microwave, consider whether you really need an all-singing, all-dancing model. Microwaves are now available that are also grills and convection ovens, but unless your kitchen is very small you probably already have a grill and an oven, so why pay for them again? If, as I do, you are going to use your microwave as a kitchen gadget, then I would advise buying the smallest and simplest one possible.

Pizza plates

Very technical pizza trays are now available with perforations to ensure a crispy base. A simple baking tray, preheated in a hot oven, will have a similar effect. However, if you are going to be dishing up a lot of pizzas, a special plate and a roller cutter make the whole business of serving much quicker and less messy.

INGREDIENTS

Most American ingredients are now readily available. The usual British terms for them have been used here, but if you should also be using an American cookery book, you will find a useful glossary of terms at the back of this book.

Throughout the book I have specified full cream milk in the recipes. Nowadays, many people prefer to use skimmed or semi-skimmed milk as an alternative. Use your own judgement about whether the substitution will adversely affect the finished dish.

I have also used vanilla extract, rather than vanilla essence throughout. Vanilla extract is now widely available and gives a preferable flavour. If you wish to use vanilla essence, halve the quantity suggested.

Variations

Many of the recipes in this book are given with variation suggestions. Once you have made a recipe for the first time, don't hesitate to experiment with changing flavours, toppings, fillings and so on – using my suggestions or your own. After all, it is through experimentation that new dishes are discovered. Have fun!

SOUPS, STARTERS AND APPETISERS

RECIPES

1
SALMON AND SWEETCORN CHOWDER
A simple milk-based chowder with a refreshing flavour and very pretty colours.

2
CHICKEN SOUP WITH DUMPLINGS
With so many possible variations on this classic recipe, here is a basic but delicious starting point.

3
PUMPKIN SOUP
Use the hollowed-out pumpkin as a serving dish for this unusual autumn soup.

4
SEAFOOD GUMBO
A thick soup, which can be varied by your choice of seafood.

5
BLACK BEAN SOUP
This soup, popularised in song, originates in Florida, introduced by Spanish settlers.

6
ORANGE SPICED NUTS
An irresistible nibble to serve with drinks at any time of day.

7
SWEETCORN FRITTERS WITH TOMATO SALSA
Crisp little sweetcorn pancakes pepped up with a tangy tomato sauce.

8
GUACAMOLE
A creamy smooth avocado dip with a certain kick. Serve with tortilla chips as a starter or with drinks.

9
PRAWNS WITH RED PEPPER SAUCE
An interesting alternative to the more traditional prawn cocktail.

10
SAVOURY PUFFS
Light choux buns with a choice of fillings make a tasty starter or buffet dish.

11
ROSEMARY CHEESE STRAWS
These light and flaky nibbles are quite irresistible.

Starters are not universally offered in American restaurants. This is partly because many meals are preceded by soup and salad. The soup tends to be served in a small cup. The salad is eaten first, rather than accompanying or being eaten after the main course. This means the salad, which can be quite substantial, takes the place of a starter.

An alternative reason could be that American portions are huge! A starter followed by a 16oz steak and an enormous baked potato could mean that one simply would not have room for dessert, and this would be a sad state of affairs!

The soups, starters and appetisers listed in this chapter are all acceptable with our more modest portions, but bear in mind that the soups tend to be quite hearty. They make an ideal light lunch, with crusty bread, but should be served in small amounts before main meals. Other starters, such as sweetcorn fritters with salsa and prawns in red pepper sauce would also make delicious snack meals, perhaps with a green salad.

PUMPKIN SOUP

Around Hallowe'en, beautiful orange pumpkins are in season.Use one to make this delicious soup. You can scoop out the flesh for the soup and either carve the shell to make a Jack O' Lantern or, as the recipe suggests, use it as the container in which you serve the soup.

SERVES: 8
PREPARATION TIME: 45 MINUTES

1 large orange pumpkin
50g (2oz) butter
1 large onion, chopped
2 stalks celery, chopped
1 clove garlic, crushed
1.5 litres (2¾pt) chicken stock
275ml (¾pt) single cream
Salt and pepper
Chopped parsley

1 Slice the top off the pumpkin, scrape out and discard the seeds, then carefully scoop out the flesh. You will need 1kg (2.2lbs) of the flesh for the soup, cut into small cubes.

2 Melt the butter in a large pan over a medium heat. Add the onion, celery and garlic and cook for about 10 minutes, until softened.

3 Add the pumpkin pieces and sauté for 5 minutes. Then add the stock and simmer until the pumpkin is soft – about 15 minutes.

4 Purée the mixture until smooth, adding the cream and seasoning to taste. Heat through gently. Warm the pumpkin shell for 10–15 minutes in an oven preheated to 180°C/350°F/Gas Mark 4. Fill with the hot soup and serve, sprinkled with parsley.

SEAFOOD GUMBO

Gumbos are heart-warming and satisfying broths that can be varied according to the ingredients you have available

SERVES: 4
PREPARATION TIME: 40 MINUTES

45ml (3tbspn) vegetable oil
50g (2oz) plain flour
225g (8oz) onion, chopped
110g (4oz) celery, thinly sliced
2 cloves garlic, crushed
Small green pepper, deseeded and chopped
2 bay leaves
850ml (1½pt) boiling water
10ml (2tspn) salt
½ bunch spring onions, thinly sliced
450g (1lb) peeled prawns
225g (8oz) crab meat, fresh or canned
About 5ml (1tspn) Tabasco sauce

1 Heat the oil in a large saucepan over a medium heat. Add the flour and cook for 2–3 minutes, until golden brown, stirring continuously.

2 Add the onion, celery, garlic, green pepper and bay leaves and cook gently for 20 minutes.

3 Carefully add the water, stirring well to mix in. Add the salt and spring onions and simmer for 5 minutes.

4 Add the prawns and crab meat and Tabasco to taste and heat through gently.

5 Serve in bowls with a little cooked rice if wished.

COOK'S TIP

For a really authentic gumbo, add sliced okra. You will find these have a slimy "sap" which seeps out as you cut. This will actually help to thicken the soup, so do not be tempted to wash it away – you will only be left with a gluey mess in your sieve.

BLACK BEAN SOUP

SERVES: 6–8
PREPARATION TIME: 2 HOURS + OVERNIGHT SOAKING

450g (1lb) dried black beans, soaked in cold water overnight
30ml (2tbspn) olive oil
50g (2oz) smoked bacon, chopped
75g (3oz) smoked ham, chopped
2 large onions, chopped
2 cloves garlic, crushed
1 large bay leaf
Pinch each of ground cloves, cayenne pepper and dried mixed herbs
About 3 litres (6pt) chicken or beef stock
30ml (2tbspn) dry sherry
Salt and pepper
Chopped spring onions

1 Heat the oil in a large saucepan over a medium heat. Add the bacon and ham and cook for 5 minutes, stirring frequently. Add the onion and garlic and cook, stirring, for a further 5 minutes.

2 Drain the beans and add to the pan with the bay leaf, cloves, cayenne, herbs and half the stock. Bring to the boil and reduce the heat to allow the mixture to simmer, uncovered.

3 Cook for about 1½ hours, or until the beans are tender. Add most of the remaining stock as the liquid evaporates.

4 Scoop out about half the beans and purée them in a food processor or blender with any remaining stock until smooth. Return to the pan. Stir in the sherry and salt and pepper to taste. Simmer for a further 20 minutes, stirring. The soup should be quite thick. Serve garnished with chopped spring onions.

ORANGE SPICED NUTS

These make a delicious change to the usual bowls of peanuts served with drinks. I have used pecans and almonds but you could try any combination of nuts, such as hazelnuts and unsalted peanuts.

MAKES: ABOUT 275G (10OZ)
PREPARATION TIME: 30 MINUTES + COOLING

25g (1oz) unsalted butter
20ml (4tspn) grated orange zest
10ml (2tspn) ground cinnamon
5ml (1tspn) ground coriander
2.5ml (1/2 tspn) cayenne pepper
275g (10oz) pecan halves and unblanched almonds
15ml (1tbspn) caster sugar
5ml (1tspn) salt

1. Melt the butter in a heavy based saucepan over a low heat. Add the orange zest, cinnamon, coriander and cayenne pepper and sizzle for 30 seconds.
2. Add the nuts. Then stir in the sugar and salt until evenly mixed. Transfer the mixture to a baking tray and spread out evenly.
3. Bake in a preheated oven 150°C/300°F/Gas Mark 2 for 20–25 minutes, stirring occasionally, until the nuts are toasted.
4. Allow the nuts to cool. Either serve slightly warm or leave until quite cold and store in an airtight container for up to 3 days.

SWEETCORN FRITTERS WITH TOMATO SALSA

SERVES: 4
PREPARATION TIME: 20 MINUTES

FRITTERS

1 large (326g or 11½ oz) can sweetcorn kernels
1 egg
Salt and pepper
About 90g (3½ oz) plain flour
Oil for frying

SALSA

15ml (1tbspn) olive oil
2 cloves garlic, crushed
2 green chillies, chopped
1 red pepper, deseeded and chopped
450g (1lb) ripe red tomatoes, peeled and chopped
Salt and pepper
15ml (1tbspn) lemon juice

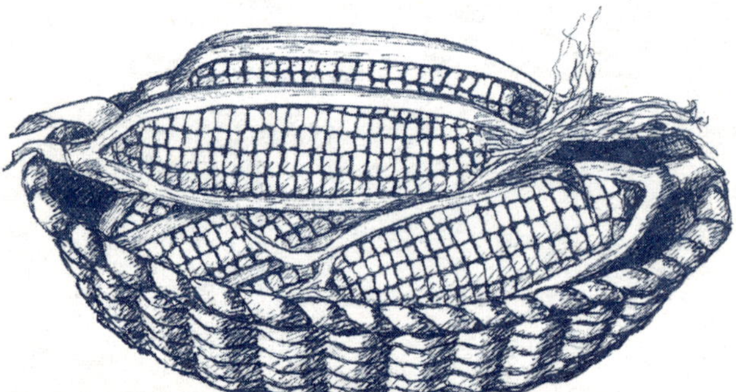

1 First make the salsa. Heat the oil in a pan over a medium heat and add the garlic. Fry for a minute, then add the chillies, red pepper and tomatoes.

2 Simmer the mixture for 5 minutes. The vegetables should retain some of their texture. Add the lemon juice and salt and pepper to taste. Keep warm.

3 Empty the entire contents of the can of sweetcorn into a bowl. Using a fork, mix in the egg and a dash of salt and pepper.

4 Now add enough flour to make a batter that will drop gently from the fork – too thick and the fritters will be stodgy, too thin and you will have sweetcorn pancakes.

5 Heat about 30ml (2tbspn) oil in a pan over a medium to high heat. Drop spoonsful of the mixture into the oil They should spread to 5cm (2 inch) rounds. When browned on the base, turn each fritter over and brown the other side. Remove the fritters from the pan and keep warm while cooking other fritters.

6 Serve 3 or 4 fritters per person with a helping of salsa.

Served without the salsa, these fritters are delicious served with bacon, eggs and tomatoes for breakfast. Or try them with sausages for an easy supper dish.

GUACAMOLE

This is a creamy avocado dip. Serve it with tortilla chips and crudités to accompany drinks or as a starter.

SERVES: 4
PREPARATION TIME: 10 MINUTES + CHILLING TIME

2 ripe avocados
15ml (1tbspn) lime or lemon juice
2 tomatoes, skinned, deseeded and finely chopped
1 small onion, finely chopped
1 red chilli, deseeded and very finely chopped
15ml (1tbspn) fresh coriander, chopped
1 clove garlic, crushed

1 Halve the avocados lengthwise and remove the stones. Scrape the flesh into a bowl and mash with a fork until quite smooth, but don't worry if there is a little texture left.

2 Add the remaining ingredients and mix well. Cover and refrigerate for an hour.

3 Mix again and serve.

COOK'S TIP

Avocado mixtures tend to discolour very quickly on the surface. For that reason, it is not advisable to make this dip more than 2 hours before you intend to serve it. Giving the dip a final stir before serving is also a good idea.

PRAWNS WITH RED PEPPER SAUCE

SERVES: 4
PREPARATION TIME: 20 MINUTES

450g (1lb) prawns, defrosted and drained weight if frozen
2 large red peppers
215ml (7.5 fl oz) mayonnaise
30ml (2tbspn) parsley, chopped
2 cloves garlic, crushed
5ml (1tspn) made-up mustard
5ml (1tspn) lemon juice

1 First grill the peppers as follows. Cut them in half and scoop out the seeds and membrane. Then place the halves, skin side up, under a hot grill and cook until the skin is charred all over. Scrape this burnt skin away and discard. Chop the pepper flesh finely.

2 Place the peppers with the mayonnaise (which can be the calorie-reduced type), parsley, garlic, mustard and lemon juice in a food processor or blender and work until quite smooth. Scrape the mixture into a bowl and fold in the prawns.

3 Serve on a bed of lettuce in ramekin dishes or scallop shells.

You will find a blender or food processor makes short work of preparing this dish. If you do not own one, cook the pepper until softened, either in boiling water or in the microwave. Then push it through a fine sieve and blend this purée with the remaining ingredients.

SAVOURY PUFFS

MAKES: 40
PREPARATION TIME: 45 MINUTES

215ml (7.5 fl oz) milk
110g (4oz) butter
2.5ml (1/2 tspn) salt
110g (4oz) plain flour, sifted on to a piece of baking parchment
2 eggs, beaten
3 egg whites

1 Heat the milk, butter and salt in a medium-sized saucepan. As soon as the mixture comes to the boil, remove it from the heat and quickly shoot in the flour. Beat until the dough leaves the sides of the pan.

2 Mix together the eggs and the egg whites and gradually add to the flour mixture, beating well between each addition. The mixture should look smooth and glossy.

3 Drop mounds of dough about the size of table tennis balls on to greased baking trays. Leave space between them to allow for puffing up.

4 Bake in a preheated oven 220°C/425°F/Gas Mark 7 for about 25 minutes until well puffed up and golden brown. Remove the trays from the oven and immediately cut a small slit in each puff to allow the steam to escape. Transfer to cooling racks and cool before filling.

SAVOURY HAM FILLING
50g (2oz) parmesan cheese, grated
50g (2oz) smoked ham, chopped
Pinch of ground nutmeg

ITALIAN FILLING
50g (2oz) sun-dried tomatoes, chopped
15ml (1tbspn) black olives, chopped
50g (2oz) full fat soft cheese

1 Blend all the ingredients for each filling together.

2 Fill the buns with the fillings. Arrange on a baking tray, cover lightly with aluminium foil, and heat in an oven preheated to 190°C/375°F/Gas Mark 5 for 10–15 minutes.

ROSEMARY CHEESE STRAWS

Rosemary is a popular herb in America and is particularly good in these tasty little nibbles. They are also delicious served with soup or a crispy salad.

MAKES: ABOUT 50 PIECES
PREPARATION TIME: 30 MINUTES

75g (3oz) parmesan cheese, finely grated
75g (3oz) cheddar cheese, finely grated
15ml (1tbspn) fresh rosemary, finely chopped
250g (9oz) puff pastry, thawed if frozen

1 Roll out the pastry on a lightly floured work surface to a rectangle 30 x 45cm (12 x 18 inches).

2 Blend the cheeses and the rosemary. Sprinkle a third of this mixture over half of the pastry and fold the uncovered pastry over the covered half. Roll out again to the 30 x 45cm (12 x 18 inches) rectangle. Repeat this process twice more to use up all the cheese mixture.

3 Now roll again to the rectangle and cut in half to make two 30 x 22.5cm (12 x 9 inch) pieces. Cut these into 1cm (1/2 inch) strips 22.5cm (9 inch) long. Twist each strip a few times.

4 Arrange the strips on baking-parchment-lined baking trays and press down the ends gently to ensure that they do not untwist.

5 Bake at 220°C/425°F/Gas Mark 7 for 8–10 minutes. Cool for about 5 minutes and then transfer carefully to cooling racks. Serve warm or at room temperature. These can be stored in an airtight tin for up to 3 days. If you wish, refresh them in a warm oven for 5 minutes before serving.

Suppers and Snacks

RECIPES

1
CHICAGO DEEP-DISH PIZZA

A thick pizza crust filled with rich tomato sauce and dripping with cheese and the toppings of your choice. No wonder this is Chicago's favourite snack.

2
THIN AND CRISPY PIZZA

If you prefer a pizza that's a little less substantial but just as full of flavour, then this is the one for you.

3
QUICK ALTERNATIVE PIZZA

The essence of a snack is that it can be quickly prepared. This frying-pan pizza fits the bill perfectly.

4
HAMBURGERS

A snack that needs no introduction but will be a very pleasant surprise to anyone who has only eaten the high-street version.

5
VEGEBURGERS

An alternative recipe that ensures vegetarians do not miss out on America's most famous snack.

6
BURGER TOPPINGS AND RELISHES

The purist might argue that nothing tops a plain burger. Try these tasty additions and make up your own mind!

7
SLOPPY JOES
As the name suggests, this is not finger food. A knife and fork are needed to tackle this hot and saucy sandwich.

8
HUSH PUPPIES
These crispy little cornmeal fritters are delicious served with a dip and an essential accompaniment to fried fish.

9
CLUB SANDWICH
A three-tiered snack combining chicken, bacon, tomatoes and lettuce in a toasted sandwich.

10
"SUBS"
French bread split open and stuffed with the fillings of your choice.

11
FRENCH TOAST
Creamy on the inside and crispy on the outside, French toast is delicious on its own, with syrup or as part of a hearty brunch.

12
EGGS BENEDICT
Crispy toasted muffins topped with poached eggs and creamy hollandaise sauce.

13
POTATO LATKES
Little potato pancakes traditionally served with apple sauce or soured cream.

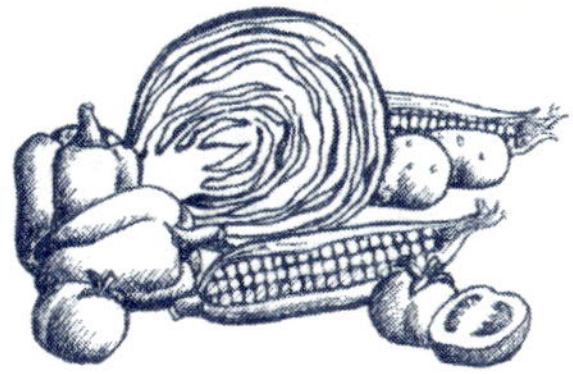

14
HOT DOGS
With onions, mustard and ketchup or completely plain, this snack is a street-food classic.

15
MACARONI AND CHEESE
This dish proves that snacks do not have to be complicated to taste good.

16
BARBECUE CHICKEN SANDWICH

Chunks of cooked chicken wrapped in a punchy barbecue sauce and packed in a toasted sesame bun.

17
RED FLANNEL HASH

A variation on the traditional corned beef hash, this recipe includes beetroot for colour, texture and flavour.

18
FRIED POTATO SKINS

Now a standard on many restaurant menus, these crisply fried potato skins filled with bacon and cheese are hard to resist.

CHICAGO DEEP-DISH PIZZA

Although pizzas did not originate in America, the Americans can certainly take the credit for popularising them, and for introducing some amazing flavours.

SERVES: 4–6
PREPARATION TIME: 1 HOUR + PROVING TIME

DOUGH
30ml (2tbspn) dried yeast
15ml (1tbspn) sugar
425ml (3/4pt) lukewarm water and milk mixed
700g (1 1/2lb) plain flour
10ml (2tspn) salt
90g (3oz) butter
3 eggs, beaten

TOMATO SAUCE
30ml (2tbspn) olive oil
1 onion, finely chopped
2 cloves garlic, crushed
3 x 420g (14 1/2 oz) cans chopped tomatoes in juice
15ml (1tbspn) sugar
15ml (1tbspn) fresh basil, chopped
60ml (4tbspn) fresh parsley, chopped
Pinch of dried oregano
10ml (2tspn) salt
Freshly ground black pepper

TO FINISH
450g (1lb) Italian sausage, sliced
225g (8oz) ham, chopped
450g (1lb) mozzarella cheese, grated
45g (1½ oz) parmesan cheese, grated

1 To make the dough, combine the yeast, sugar and 75ml (5tbspn) of the warm water and milk mixture in a small bowl and leave for 15 minutes, until the liquid begins to froth.

2 Sift the flour and salt into a large bowl and rub in the butter to give the appearance of fine breadcrumbs. Make a well in the centre and add the yeast mixture, the beaten eggs and the remaining warm water and milk. With a wooden spoon, begin to bring the mixture together and then work with your hands to make a rough dough.

3 Turn the dough on to a floured work surface and knead until smooth, adding more flour if required. Return to a lightly floured bowl, cover with a clean tea towel and leave in a warm place until doubled in size – about 1½ hours.

4 Meanwhile make the tomato sauce. Heat the oil in a large pan over a medium heat. Add the onion and garlic and cook for 5 minutes. Stir in the remaining ingredients, bring to the boil, reduce the heat and simmer gently, uncovered, for about 1½ hours, stirring occasionally until the mixture is very thick.

5 Grease two 22cm (9 inch) round pans, about 5cm (2 inches) deep. Knead the dough well to return it to its original size and divide into two equally sized pieces. Roll each piece out to a circle about 27cm ($10\frac{1}{2}$ inches) in diameter. Line each pan with dough, pressing it halfway up the sides. Leave them in a warm place for 15 minutes.

6 Take half the mozzarella cheese and sprinkle it evenly on the two bases. Spread the tomato sauce over the cheese, dividing it equally between the two bases. Divide the sausage and ham between the two pizzas and top with the remaining mozzarella and parmesan.

7 Bake the pizzas in an oven heated to 200°C/400°F/Gas Mark 6 for 25–30 minutes, until crisp and golden. Cut each pizza into 4 to serve.

To make a delicious home-made pizza is quite time consuming but there are a number of shortcuts you can take to speed up the process:

Use a bread dough mix for the base.

Use a ready made tomato sauce.

Buy ready grated cheese: mozzarella and parmesan are both available like this in most large supermarkets.

Make double the quantity of mix, it hardly takes any longer, and freeze it, either before or after cooking.

THIN AND CRISPY PIZZA

The world can be divided into those who like their pizzas thick and fluffy, and those who prefer them thin and crispy. If you fall into the latter group, this is the recipe for you.

SERVES: 4
PREPARATION TIME: 1 HOUR + PROVING TIME

DOUGH
275g (8oz) plain flour
5ml (1tspn) salt
25g (1oz) butter
10ml (2tspn) sugar
225ml (8 fl oz) lukewarm water
15ml (1tbspn) dried yeast

SAUCE
15ml (1tbspn) olive oil
1 small onion, finely chopped
1 clove garlic, crushed
300ml (½pt) passata
15ml (1tbspn) tomato purée
15ml (1tbspn) fresh basil, chopped
5ml (1tspn) dried oregano
Salt and pepper

TOPPING
225g (8oz) mozzarella cheese, grated
275g (10oz) salami, Italian sausage, ham or a mixture
1 green pepper, finely sliced
Olives (optional)

1 Sift the flour and salt into a bowl and rub in the butter until the mixture resembles fine breadcrumbs.

2 Mix the sugar, yeast and 60ml (4tbspn) of the lukewarm water in a small bowl. Leave in a warm place for 10 minutes. Make a well in the centre of the flour and add the yeast mixture and remaining water. Mix to form a rough dough.

3 Turn the dough on to a floured work surface and knead until smooth. Return to a lightly floured bowl, cover with a clean tea towel, and leave in a warm place for about an hour, until doubled in size.

4 Meanwhile make the topping. Heat the oil in a pan over a medium heat. Add the onion and garlic and cook for about 10 minutes, until softened and lightly coloured. Add the remaining ingredients, bring to the boil, reduce the heat and simmer for 45 minutes.

5 Knead the dough until it returns to its original size and, on a lightly floured work surface, roll out to as large a circle as your biggest baking tray (and oven!) can take. Transfer the dough carefully on to this tray, having first greased it well with olive oil. You may have to reshape the dough a bit once it is on the tray as it can stretch in transit. If you do not have a large baking tray, you may find it easier to divide the dough into two pieces and make two smaller pizzas. Leave the dough in a warm place for 15 minutes.

6 Spread the sauce over the dough and cover with your choice of meat, pepper and olives, if using. Cover with cheese.

7 Bake in an oven preheated to 230°C/450°F/Gas Mark 8 for 15–20 minutes, until crisp and golden. Serve cut into wedges.

QUICK ALTERNATIVE PIZZA

SERVES: 2
PREPARATION TIME: 30 MINUTES

BASE
225g (8oz) self-raising flour
Pinch of salt and pepper
30ml (2tbspn) olive oil
Water to mix

SAUCE
60ml (4tbspn) passata
30ml (2tbspn) tomato purée
15ml (1tbspn) fresh basil, chopped

TOPPING
110g (4oz) mozzarella cheese, grated
50g (2oz) ham, chopped
Olive oil for frying

1 Sift the flour into a bowl with the salt and pepper. Make a well in the centre and add the olive oil and enough water to make a soft but not sticky dough.

2 Roll out the dough on a lightly floured work surface to a circle about 25cm (10 inches) in diameter or to fit the base of your largest frying pan.

3 Heat 15ml (1tbspn) of olive oil in a frying pan over a medium heat. Carefully place the circle of dough in the pan and cook over a low heat for 5 minutes.

4 Turn the partly cooked dough out on to a large plate, heat another 15ml (1tbspn) of olive oil in the pan and slide the pizza base back into the pan, cooked side up.

5 Mix together the sauce ingredients and spread over the cooked surface. Cook for a further 5 minutes.

6 Top with ham and cheese and slide the pan under a preheated hot grill for 4–5 minutes, to melt and brown the cheese. Serve at once.

HAMBURGERS

SERVES: 4–6
PREPARATION TIME: 15 MINUTES

700g (1½lb) minced beef, about 10–15% fat
Salt
Freshly ground pepper

1 Place the meat in a bowl and gradually mix in the salt and pepper to your taste. Do not over mix as this will toughen the meat.

2 Shape the meat into 4–6 patties about 2.5cm (1 inch) thick. You can do this by hand or invest in a small plastic burger press. These are inexpensive and available from kitchen shops and larger supermarkets. Using a press will give the burgers a slightly tighter texture but they will lose some of their "homemade" appearance.

3 Grill or barbecue the burgers under a medium to high heat for 3–6 minutes on each side, depending how rare you like your meat.

4 Serve the burgers in buns with relish – you will find some ideas on the following pages – and your choice of lettuce, tomatoes, dill pickles and cheese.

VEGEBURGERS

There is no reason why vegetarians should not enjoy burgers. This recipe is delicious served in a bun with the relishes suggested for hamburgers.

SERVES: 6
PREPARATION TIME: 40 MINUTES

60ml (4tbspn) olive oil
2 onions, finely chopped
1 clove garlic, crushed
2 celery stalks, finely chopped
1 carrot, grated
Fresh herbs to taste, chopped
30ml (2tbspn) wholemeal plain flour
215ml (7.5fl oz) water
1 vegetable stock cube
30ml (2tbspn) soy sauce
225g (8oz) wholemeal breadcrumbs
450g (1lb) mixed nuts, roughly ground
Salt and pepper
Oil for frying

1 Heat the oil in a pan over a medium heat. Add the onion and garlic and cook for 5–10 minutes, until soft and golden. Add the celery and carrot and cook for a further 5 minutes. Add the herbs.

2 Stir in the flour and cook for 2 minutes. Slowly add the water, stirring constantly, and heat until thickened. Add the crumbled stock cube and soy sauce. Mix in the breadcrumbs and nuts and season to taste. Leave to cool.

3 Divide the mixture into 12 even-sized pieces and shape into burgers about 1cm ($^{1}/_{2}$ inch) thick.

4 Heat the oil in a pan, either on the stove or over a barbecue and cook the burgers for 10 minutes on each side.

Handle these burgers carefully as they are quite crumbly. It is wise to cook them in a pan over the barbecue rather than directly on the rack.

BURGER TOPPINGS AND RELISHES

CREAMY MUSTARD DRESSING
15ml (1tbspn) Dijon mustard
150ml ($^{1}/_{4}$pt) mayonnaise
10ml (2tspn) runny honey
10ml (2tspn) chopped chives
Salt and pepper

1 Mix the mustard and mayonnaise together in a small bowl.

2 Mix in the honey and chives and season to taste.

TOMATO RELISH

4 large tomatoes, skinned and deseeded
1 small onion, finely chopped
15ml (1tbspn) fresh parsley, chopped
15ml (1tbspn) fresh coriander, chopped
1 small green chilli, finely chopped
15ml (1tbspn) lemon juice
Salt and pepper

1 Chop the tomatoes into very small cubes. Mix with the onion, herbs, chilli and lemon juice and season to taste.

2 Leave in a cool place for 1 hour to allow the flavours to develop.

BLUE CHEESE DRESSING

110g (4oz) blue cheese, crumbled
150ml (1/4pt) mayonnaise
Freshly ground black pepper

Mash the blue cheese in a bowl with a fork. Gradually stir in the mayonnaise but don't mix too thoroughly as it is nice to find some chunks of cheese in the relish. Add pepper to taste.

SLOPPY JOES

A sort of hot sandwich made from minced beef in a tomato sauce, this is best served in a toasted burger bun.

SERVES: 4
PREPARATION TIME: 55 MINUTES

450g (1lb) minced beef
1 onion, finely chopped
1 small green pepper, deseeded and finely chopped
50g (2oz) mushrooms, finely chopped
225g (8oz) passata
15ml (1tbspn) tomato purée
15ml (1tbspn) Worcestershire sauce
Salt and pepper
4 burger buns

1 Heat the beef and onion in a heavy based pan over a high heat, stirring and breaking down the lumps. The meat will begin to sizzle and release its fat.

2 Add the green pepper, mushrooms, passata, purée and Worcestershire sauce. Mix well, reduce the heat and simmer for 45 minutes.

3 Add salt and pepper to taste.

4 Slit the burger buns and toast the cut sides under a hot grill. Arrange the bases on four plates, top with equal portions of the meat mix and arrange the lids, at an angle, on top.

HUSH PUPPIES

The story goes that cowboys used to make these little fried dumplings over the camp stove and throw them to the camp dogs to stop them barking – hence the name! They are an essential accompaniment to fried catfish, but if this does not appear regularly on your menu, try them with sausages or bacon.

SERVES: 4
PREPARATION TIME: 15 MINUTES

110g (4oz) cornmeal
40g (1½oz) self-raising flour
5ml (1tspn) baking powder
Pinch of salt
4 spring onions, chopped
1 egg
About 75ml (5tbspn) milk
Oil for frying

1 Sieve together the cornmeal, flour, baking powder and salt into a large bowl. Stir in the onions and egg and add enough milk to form a soft dough.

2 Heat about 2cm (¾ inch) of oil in a deep, heavy based saucepan until hot enough to brown a piece of bread in a few seconds.

3 Drop spoonsful of the mixture into the oil and fry, turning, until golden brown – about 2½–3 minutes. Drain on kitchen paper and serve.

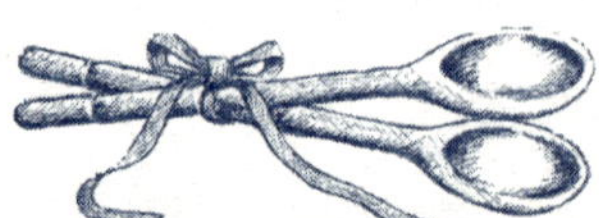

CLUB SANDWICH

Probably America's most popular sandwich, this three-tiered stack makes a substantial snack. Serve with fries for a hearty meal.

SERVES: 1
PREPARATION TIME: 10 MINUTES

3 slices of bread, toasted on both sides
Crisp lettuce leaves
Mayonnaise
Thin slices of cooked turkey or chicken
Thinly sliced tomatoes
Crisply grilled bacon rashers – smoked streaky works well
Salt and pepper
Cocktail sticks

1 Lay a piece of toast on a chopping board and spread with mayonnaise. Top with a lettuce leaf and cover with turkey or chicken. Season. Cover with a second piece of toast.

2 Spread the second piece of toast with mayonnaise. Cover with lettuce, tomato slices and bacon rashers. Season.

3 Spread the last piece of toast with mayonnaise and place it, mayonnaise side down, on top of the bacon.

4 Press down lightly and cut into quarters, through the diagonals. Still holding, push a cocktail stick through each quarter, to prevent them from falling apart. Cocktail sticks with frills on the end look particularly attractive when serving this dish. If you use plain sticks, remember to warn people eating the sandwiches that they are there – sometimes the end can disappear into the top layer of bread.

"SUBS"

Subs are long French sticks, filled with a variety of good things, and actually sold by the foot in some American fast-food restaurants. The fillings below are merely suggestions to get you started. You can make a sub with one filling, or have different ones along the length.

French stick, split along the top, but not quite through to the base, lightly buttered
Your choice of:
Sliced salami and coleslaw
Thinly sliced ham, sliced hardboiled eggs, chopped gherkins and mayonnaise
Sliced cheese, sliced tomatoes and finely sliced onions
Shredded roast chicken, potato salad and lettuce
Salt beef (hot if wished) and dill pickles
Scrambled eggs and crisply cooked bacon, chopped
Pastrami, crisp lettuce and American mustard
Tuna, sweetcorn and mayonnaise
Smoked salmon, soured cream and freshly chopped dill
Prawns, chopped cucumber and lemon mayonnaise

1 Pack the filling or fillings of your choice into the bread.

2 Cut into lengths as required. Wrap with napkins to serve.

Be generous with the fillings – they should be bursting out of the bread! Because of this, it's a good idea to use mayonnaise, coleslaw or mustard in the filling to act as a kind of "glue".

FRENCH TOAST

This is a more exciting version of "eggy bread". It can be made up to stage three and held in the refrigerator overnight.

SERVES: 6
PREPARATION TIME: 30 MINUTES + STANDING TIME

1 small French stick
2 eggs
75g (3oz) caster sugar
Grated zest of 1 lemon
275ml (1/2pt) full cream milk
45ml (3tbspn) cream
2.5ml (1/2tspn) ground cinnamon
Pinch grated nutmeg
Vegetable oil for frying

1 Whisk together the eggs, sugar, lemon, milk, cream and spices.

2 Cut the French stick into about 12–16 slices, 2cm (3/4 inch) thick. Dip these slices into the egg mixture, turning until thoroughly soaked, and transfer to a large, shallow dish. After dipping all the slices, pour over any excess liquid.

3 Cover the dish and leave to stand for at least 30 minutes.

4 Heat a little oil in a heavy based frying pan over a medium to high heat. Add as many slices as will fit and quickly brown on one side. Turn and brown the other side before transferring to a baking tray. Treat the remaining slices in the same way.

5 Bake the toasts in a preheated oven 200°C/400°F/Gas Mark 6 for 10–15 minutes, until well puffed up. Serve piping hot with syrup, jam or fruit.

EGGS BENEDICT

English muffins are hugely popular in America and form the base of this classic egg dish, which makes a tasty supper or a hearty brunch.

SERVES: 2 AS A LIGHT MEAL OR 4 AS A SNACK OR PART OF BRUNCH
PREPARATION TIME: 20 MINUTES

2 English muffins, halved
4 thick slices of ham or 4 thick back bacon rashers
4 eggs
2 egg yolks
Pinch of mustard powder
225g (8oz) unsalted butter
30ml (2tbspn) lemon juice
Salt and pepper

1 Toast the muffins on the cut side and place in a warm oven.

2 Grill the ham or bacon and poach the eggs. Place the meat on the muffins and top with the eggs.

3 To make the sauce, place the egg yolks, mustard powder and lemon juice in a bowl over a saucepan of simmering water. In a small bowl, over a low heat, or in a bowl in the microwave on defrost, melt the butter, but do not allow it to sizzle.

4 Whisk the egg-yolk mixture and very slowly drizzle in the melted butter, whisking all the time. Continue to beat until the mixture thickens.

5 Arrange the topped muffins on plates and pour the sauce over. Serve at once.

MACARONI AND CHEESE

SERVES: 4
PREPARATION TIME: 55 MINUTES

110g (4oz) macaroni
25g (1oz) butter
1 small onion, finely chopped
15ml (1tbspn) plain flour
215ml (7.5fl oz) full fat milk
1 egg, beaten
5ml (1tspn) salt
Pinch of pepper
150g (5oz) cheddar cheese, grated

1 Cook the macaroni in plenty of salted boiling water for about 10 minutes, until just tender. Drain, rinse under cold water and allow to cool, stirring occasionally to prevent pieces sticking together.

2 Meanwhile melt the butter in a pan over a medium heat. Add the onion and fry gently for 5 minutes. Add the flour and cook for 2 minutes, stirring. Whisk in the milk and bring to the boil, stirring, until the mixture thickens.

3 Remove the pan from the heat, allow to cool for 5 minutes, then beat in the egg and season to taste.

4 Stir in 110g (4oz) of the grated cheese and the macaroni and transfer the mixture to a greased oven-proof dish. Sprinkle with the remaining cheese.

5 Bake in an oven preheated to 190°C/375°F/Gas Mark 5 for 30 minutes, until golden brown and bubbling.

BARBECUE CHICKEN SANDWICH

SERVES: 4
PREPARATION TIME: 45 MINUTES

450g (1lb) cooked chicken meat, diced into 1cm (1/2 inch) cubes
4 burger buns
2 large onions, chopped
2 cloves garlic, crushed
30ml (2tbspn) vegetable oil
75g (3oz) soft dark brown sugar
45ml (3tbspn) red wine vinegar
30ml (2tbspn) Worcestershire sauce
420g (14 1/2 oz) can chopped tomatoes in juice
30ml (2tbspn) tomato purée
5ml (1tspn) mustard powder
Salt and pepper

1 Heat the oil in a pan over a medium heat. Add the onion and garlic and cook for 5 minutes.

2 Add the sugar, vinegar, Worcestershire sauce, tomatoes, tomato purée, mustard powder and seasoning to taste. Simmer, uncovered, for about 30 minutes, until very thick.

3 Purée the mixture in a liquidiser or food processor or push through a sieve.

4 Place the diced chicken meat in a saucepan and add enough sauce to bind. Heat through gently.

5 Meanwhile split open the buns and toast on the cut sides. Place the bases on plates, top evenly with the hot sauce and top with the lids. Serve at once.

Fish and Shellfish

RECIPES

1
DEVILLED CRAB

Crab meat in a spicy sauce with a crispy cheese and breadcrumb topping.

2
BAKED SALMON

A classic way of adding succulence and flavour to this popular fish.

3
PRAWN AND HAM JAMBALAYA

A rice-based supper dish flavoured with green pepper, having a punchy kick from cayenne pepper and Tabasco.

4
SEAFOOD AU GRATIN

A selection of seafood bound in a rich cheese sauce.

5
GRILLED TUNA STEAKS

A delicious way of preparing fish steaks for the grill or barbecue.

6
MARYLAND CRABCAKES WITH TARTARE OR DILL SAUCE

Delicious crisply fried crabcakes with a choice of sauces.

7
LOBSTER NEWBURG

Some would argue that nothing can improve on plain lobster – try this recipe before you agree with them!

8
CREOLE PRAWNS

Fresh, colourful vegetables are cooked with prawns for this Southern-style dish.

9
POPCORN SHRIMPS

Crisply battered prawns served with a tangy remoulade sauce.

10
CRAB COBBLER

Crab meat in a thick cheese sauce topped with a crispy "cobblestone" crust.

11
BAKED STUFFED RED SNAPPER

A whole fish, stuffed and cooked. You can vary the stuffing as you wish.

12
OYSTERS ROCKEFELLER

This is simply one of those dishes that everybody should try, at least once.

America is rich in lakes and rivers and has a varied coastline on two oceans, so it is not surprising that many classic American dishes include fish and shellfish. Originally, catching fish was a way of life for many settlers, often taught by native American fishermen. Nowadays, fishing tends to be a sport, rather than an essential for providing food. The variety of fish and shellfish on offer to the Americans is amazing, largely due to the variety of climate and the choice of salt and fresh water. In the warmer Atlantic waters of the south, flounders, red snapper and swordfish flourish, while the Pacific shores are renowned for such fish as blue-fin tuna, Chinook salmon and sea bass. Trout and catfish inhabit the inland rivers, while the Great Lakes contribute perch and lake trout.

Oysters, clams, mussels, scallops, abalone, shrimps and lobsters are just some of the shellfish available, though these are not necessarily the varieties familiar to us. What Americans call shrimps we would term prawns and there would be a friendly rivalry as to which was better, the American king crab or the British Cromer crab. The king crab has incredibly long claws, but I would say the Cromer crab has it beaten for flavour. Lobsters come in many varieties but it is generally agreed that those from the waters around Maine are best, and this area also provides the most delicious mussels.

With so many different fish and shellfish to choose from, it is interesting that Americans tend to cook them in fairly simple ways. When fish is fresh, there is no better cooking method than grilling, and chilled shellfish merely requires a classic mayonnaise accompaniment to turn it into a sumptuous meal. Seafood soups and casseroles are popular, as is lightly breaded fried fish. We are not able to buy all the native American seafood, but Maine lobsters are now air freighted across the Atlantic and tuna steaks and red snapper are appearing on the fishmonger's slab and in the freezer cabinets of major supermarket chains.

DEVILLED CRAB

SERVES: 4
PREPARATION TIME: 40 MINUTES

50g (2oz) butter
50g (2oz) onion, grated
10g (1/2oz) plain flour
150ml (1/4pt) single cream
5ml (1tspn) made mustard
5ml (1tspn) Worcestershire sauce
15ml (1tbspn) dry sherry
5ml (1tspn) salt
Pinch cayenne pepper
15ml (1tbspn) fresh parsley, chopped
450g (1lb) crab meat, light and dark meat mixed
50g (2oz) cheddar cheese, grated
25g (1oz) fresh white breadcrumbs

1 Heat the butter in a saucepan over a moderate heat until bubbling. Add the onion and cook gently until soft and just coloured.

2 Mix in the flour and cook, stirring, for 1 minute. Add the cream, mustard, Worcestershire sauce, sherry, salt, pepper and parsley.

3 Slowly bring to the boil and simmer for 2 minutes. Cool.

4 Mix in the crab meat. Lightly grease 4 individual dishes – scallop-shaped ones look good – and divide the mixture between them.

5 Mix the cheese and breadcrumbs together and sprinkle over the crab meat mixture. Bake at 220°C/425°F/Gas Mark 7 for 15–20 minutes, until piping hot and golden and crispy on top. Serve at once, garnished with slices of lemon.

BAKED SALMON

Much of the salmon available in our supermarkets is farmed and, although moist, it sometimes lacks flavour. This recipe adds delicious flavours and even more succulence.

SERVES: 4
PREPARATION TIME: 30 MINUTES + MARINATION TIME

15ml (1tbspn) vegetable oil
1 small onion, finely chopped
2 cloves garlic, crushed
30ml (2tbspn) fresh herbs, chopped: basil, thyme, rosemary, parsley and tarragon are a good combination
45ml (3tbspn) dry sherry
45ml (3tbspn) lemon or lime juice
2.5ml (1/2 tspn) Tabasco sauce
10ml (2tspn) Worcestershire sauce
4 salmon steaks

1 Heat the oil in a pan over a medium heat. Add the onion and garlic and cook for about 10 minutes until softened but not coloured.

2 Remove the pan from the heat. Add the herbs, sherry, lemon or lime juice, Tabasco and Worcestershire sauce. Mix well.

3 Arrange the steaks in a shallow dish so that they do not overlap. Pour over the marinade, cover and chill for at least 12 but preferably 24 hours.

4 Place each piece of fish in a square of foil and wrap loosely. Place on a baking tray and cook at 180°C/350°F/Gas Mark 4 for 15 minutes. Serve hot or cold.

PRAWN AND HAM JAMBALAYA

SERVES: 4
PREPARATION TIME: 35 MINUTES

30ml (2tbspn) vegetable oil
2 medium onions, finely chopped
2 sticks celery, finely chopped
1 small green pepper, deseeded and finely chopped
2 cloves garlic, crushed
225g (8oz) long-grain rice
About 570ml (1pt) water
2 bay leaves
Salt and pepper
5ml (1tspn) cayenne pepper
2.5ml (½tspn) Tabasco sauce
225g (8oz) shelled prawns
110g (4oz) ham, cut into 1cm (½ inch) cubes

1 Place the oil in a large, heavy based saucepan over a medium heat. Add the onion, celery, green pepper and garlic. Stir and add the rice. Cook, stirring occasionally, for 5 minutes, until the rice starts to brown and the vegetables begin to soften.

2 Add about a quarter of the water and bring to the boil. Add the prawns, ham and seasonings.

3 Add the remaining water and bring to the boil. Stir once, cover and reduce the heat. Simmer until the rice is cooked and most of the water has been absorbed. This should take about 20 minutes.

4 Adjust the seasonings as required and serve immediately.

SEAFOOD AU GRATIN

SERVES: 4
PREPARATION TIME: 35 MINUTES

50g (2oz) butter
50g (2oz) plain flour
2.5ml (1/2 tspn) salt
Pinch of white pepper
215ml (7.5fl oz) full cream milk
225g (8oz) mature cheddar cheese, grated
60ml (4tbspn) dry sherry
Pinch of mustard powder
450g (1lb) mixed seafood: crab meat, prawns, mussels, scallops etc.

1 In a pan over a medium to high heat, melt the butter until bubbling. Add the flour, salt and pepper and cook, stirring, for 2 minutes.

2 Gradually beat in the milk until a smooth paste is formed. (Swift action with a whisk can usually remedy any lumps at this stage.) Bring to the boil, stirring, until a very thick sauce is formed. Stir in most of the cheese.

3 The sauce will now be very thick. Gradually stir in the sherry and mustard.

4 Spread half the sauce over the base of a greased oven-proof dish and sprinkle evenly with the seafood. Cover with the remaining sauce and sprinkle with the rest of the cheese.

5 Bake in an oven preheated to 200°C/400°F/Gas Mark 6 for 20 minutes, until bubbling and golden. Serve with crusty bread and a green salad.

GRILLED TUNA STEAKS

Tuna steaks are readily available in the United States and are becoming much more common on fish counters everywhere. Tuna has a firm, almost meaty texture, which makes it ideal for marinating and grilling. Swordfish can be substituted for the tuna.

SERVES: 4
PREPARATION TIME: 1 HOUR 10 MINUTES

Juice of 2 lemons
150ml (1/4pt) olive oil
1 clove garlic, crushed
1 small onion, very finely chopped
15ml (1tbspn) fresh coriander, finely chopped
Salt and pepper
4 tuna steaks about 2.5cm (1 inch) thick

1 Combine all the ingredients except the fish into a marinade.

2 Pour a little of this marinade into a large, shallow dish. Lay the tuna steaks on to this in one layer and pour the remaining marinade over. Marinate at room temperature for about 1 hour.

3 Preheat the grill to medium–high and cook the tuna for 5–7 minutes on each side, basting with the marinade.

COOK'S TIP

This dish is even more delicious if cooked over a barbecue. Cook the marinated fish steaks over a preheated barbecue for about 4–5 minutes on each side.

MARYLAND CRABCAKES WITH TARTARE OR DILL SAUCE

SERVES: 4
PREPARATION TIME: 15 MINUTES + CHILLING TIME

1 egg
30ml (2tbspn) double cream
5ml (1tspn) made mustard
5ml (1tspn) Worcestershire sauce
Ground black pepper
1 spring onion, finely chopped
5ml (1tspn) fresh parsley, finely chopped
60ml (4tbspn) mayonnaise
450g (1lb) crab meat
75g (3oz) fresh white breadcrumbs
Oil for frying

1 Lightly whisk the egg in a large bowl. Add the cream, mustard, Worcestershire sauce and pepper to taste. Mix well.

2 Add the onion, parsley and mayonnaise and blend well.

3 Fold in the crab meat and divide the mixture evenly into 4 parts. Carefully form these into cakes – hands are the best tools for this. Gently press the cakes into the breadcrumbs to coat evenly.

4 Place the cakes on a plate, cover with cling film and chill for at least 2 hours.

5 Heat the oil in a large, heavy based frying pan over a medium heat. Add the cakes and fry for 3–4 minutes on each side, until golden brown. Drain on kitchen paper and serve with the sauce of your choice.

TARTARE SAUCE

15ml (1tbspn) white wine vinegar
5ml (1tspn) made mustard
Salt and pepper
Dash of Tabasco sauce
150ml (1/4pt) mayonnaise
4 spring onions, finely chopped
30ml (2tbspn) dill pickles, finely chopped
15ml (1tbspn) chives, chopped
15ml (1tbspn) capers, chopped

1 In a bowl mix the vinegar, mustard, salt, pepper and Tabasco. Blend with the mayonnaise.

2 Fold in the onions, dill pickles, chives and capers and mix until well blended.

3 Cover and chill for at least 1 hour before serving.

DILL SAUCE

150ml (1/4pt) crème fraîche
150ml (1/4pt) soured cream
15ml (1tbspn) fresh dill, chopped
15ml (1tbspn) fresh parsley, chopped

1 Gently mix the crème fraîche and soured cream together in a small bowl. Fold in the herbs.

2 Cover and chill for 1 hour before serving.

LOBSTER NEWBURG

In America lobsters are plentiful and relatively cheap. Here they are becoming more widely available, so treat yourself to this classic dish, invented by a New York chef in the late nineteenth century. You may find two smaller lobsters are a better price than one large one.

SERVES: 4
PREPARATION TIME: 25 MINUTES

1 cooked lobster of 700–900g (1½–2lb)
50g (2oz) unsalted butter
150ml (¼pt) double cream
60ml (4tbspn) dry sherry
Dash of Tabasco sauce
Salt and pepper
2 egg yolks

1 Remove the meat from the lobster and cut into chunks or slices. You will find that this is a process that becomes much quicker with practice. Retain the halved shells for serving if wished.

2 Melt the butter in a heavy based saucepan over a low heat. Add the lobster and heat through gently, stirring.

3 Add the cream and sherry and bring to the boil. Simmer, uncovered, until reduced by half. Add the Tabasco and seasoning to taste and reduce the heat to very low.

4 Lightly beat the egg yolks and add a few spoonsful of the warm sauce. Stir this mix back into the bulk of the sauce and cook for 3–4 minutes, stirring, until the sauce has slightly thickened. Do not allow the mixture to boil, or you will have scrambled eggs.

5 To serve, divide the mixture into 4 portions.

CREOLE PRAWNS

In America what we know as prawns would be sold as shrimps, and however large they are, shrimps they remain.

SERVES: 4–6
PREPARATION TIME: 25 MINUTES

75ml (3tbspn) olive oil
2 medium onions, finely chopped
2 cloves garlic, crushed
1 small green pepper, deseeded and chopped
1 small red pepper, deseeded and chopped
3 celery stalks, chopped
450g (1lb) ripe red tomatoes, peeled and chopped
2.5ml (1/2 tspn) dried thyme
900g (2lb) prawns, defrosted and drained if frozen
Generous pinch of cayenne pepper
Salt
Fresh parsley, chopped

1 Heat the oil in a pan over a medium heat. Add the onions and garlic and cook, stirring, for 5 minutes, until softened but not coloured.

2 Add the peppers, celery, tomatoes and thyme and bring to the boil. Cover, reduce the heat and simmer gently for 10 minutes.

3 Add the prawns, cayenne and a dash of salt and cook gently for a further 5 minutes.

4 Sprinkle with chopped parsley and serve on a bed of rice or with crusty bread.

POPCORN SHRIMPS

Small prawns seasoned, dipped in batter and fried are a New Orleans dish. Serve them with a spicy mayonnaise for a snack or starter, or with green salad and fries for a main meal.

SERVES: 2–3 AS A MAIN COURSE OR 4–6 AS A STARTER
PREPARATION TIME: 30 MINUTES + STANDING TIME

450g (1lb) prawns – weight after defrosting and draining, if frozen
30ml (2tbspn) plain flour
2.5ml (1/2tspn) paprika
2.5ml (1/2tspn) salt
Pinch ground bay leaf
Pinch black pepper
Pinch cayenne pepper

BATTER
110g (4oz) plain flour
Pinch of salt
1 egg
150ml (1/4pt) full cream milk
Oil for deep frying

1 First make the batter. Sift the flour and salt into a bowl, make a well in the centre and add the egg yolk. Gradually beat in the milk to make a smooth batter. Whisk the egg white until stiff and fold into the batter. Leave to stand for 1 hour.

2 Meanwhile flavour the prawns. Mix together the flour and seasonings and toss the prawns in this to coat evenly. Drop into the batter.

3 Heat the oil in a deep, heavy pan or deep-fat fryer to about 180°C/350°F.

4 Scoop out the prawns from the batter using a slotted spoon. Drop some of the prawns into the hot oil, trying to keep them as separate as possible. Don't worry – some will certainly stick together. You are trying to achieve bite-sized pieces, not individually battered prawns.

5 Cook until golden and crisp. Drain on kitchen paper and keep warm while frying the remaining prawns. Serve with remoulade sauce.

REMOULADE SAUCE

275ml (1/2pt) mayonnaise
15ml (1tbspn) drained gherkins, finely chopped
5ml (1tspn) made mustard
5ml (1tspn) capers, chopped
5ml (1tspn) fresh parsley, chopped
5ml (1tspn) fresh tarragon, chopped
15ml (1tbspn) dry sherry
3 anchovy fillets, drained and finely chopped

Simply blend together all the ingredients and chill until required.

CRAB COBBLER

SERVES: 4
PREPARATION TIME: 60 MINUTES

BASE

50g (2oz) butter
1 small green pepper, deseeded and sliced
1 medium onion, finely chopped
50g (2oz) plain flour
275ml (1/2pt) milk
75g (3oz) cheddar cheese, grated
Pinch of mustard powder
2 large tomatoes, peeled and chopped
275g (10oz) crab meat
Dash of Worcestershire sauce
Salt and pepper

TOPPING

110g (4oz) plain flour
Salt and pepper
10ml (2tspn) baking powder
50g (2oz) margarine
50g (2oz) cheddar cheese, grated
Milk to mix

1 First make the base. Melt the butter in a pan over a medium heat. Add the green pepper and onion and cook gently for 10 minutes, until softened. Stir in the flour and cook for 2 minutes.

2 Remove the pan from the heat and slowly add the milk, stirring continuously. Return to the heat and slowly bring to the boil, stirring, until the mixture is thick.

3 Add the cheese and mustard powder. Stir in the tomatoes, crab meat and Worcestershire sauce and season to taste. Turn into an oven-proof dish.

4 To make the topping, sift the flour, seasoning and baking powder into a bowl. Rub in the margarine to make a mix resembling fine breadcrumbs. Mix in the cheese. Bind with milk to make a soft but not sticky dough. If the mixture is too wet, you will not achieve the cobblestone look of the dish's name. Roll the dough into about 15 small balls and place on top of the crab mixture.

5 Bake in an oven preheated to 220°C/425°F/Gas Mark 7 for 20 minutes, until the mixture is bubbling and the topping is well risen and golden brown.

Prawns, flaked white fish or any seafood combination can be used in this dish instead of the crab meat.

BAKED STUFFED RED SNAPPER

SERVES: 4
PREPARATION TIME: 1 HOUR 30 MINUTES

1 large red snapper, cleaned and descaled
Olive oil
Salt and pepper

STUFFING
25g (1oz) butter
1 small onion, finely chopped
2 stalks celery, finely chopped
110g (4oz) bacon, finely chopped
75g (3oz) mushrooms, finely chopped
110g (4oz) fresh white breadcrumbs
5ml (1tspn) fresh parsley, chopped
Salt and pepper
1 egg, beaten

1 First make the stuffing. Melt the butter in a pan over a medium heat. Add the onion and celery and cook for 5 minutes. Add the bacon and mushrooms and cook, stirring, for a further 5 minutes.

2 Turn this mixture into a bowl and mix with the remaining ingredients to make a firm stuffing.

3 Brush the fish with olive oil and sprinkle with salt and pepper. Place in a greased baking dish.

4 Spoon the stuffing into the fish but do not pack too tightly – remember it will expand slightly when cooking. Secure the opening with a cocktail stick. Any excess stuffing can be rolled into small balls and placed around the fish. Cut three slits in the back of the fish about 1cm (1/2 inch) deep, to aid even cooking.

5 Cover the dish with foil and bake at 180°C/350°F/Gas Mark 4 for 50–60 minutes, until tender.

6 To serve, lift the fillet off the top and cut in two. Serve with a portion of the stuffing. Turn the fish over and repeat.

OYSTERS ROCKEFELLER

SERVES: 4
PREPARATION TIME: 30 MINUTES

75g (3oz) butter
2 large bunches spring onions, finely chopped
450g (1lb) fresh spinach, very finely chopped or
675g (1½lb) frozen chopped spinach, defrosted and thoroughly drained
1 large bunch fresh parsley, finely chopped
25g (1oz) fresh white breadcrumbs
2.5ml (½tspn) salt
30ml (2tbspn) Pernod, or similarly flavoured alcohol
Dash of Tabasco sauce
24 oysters on the half shell
Rock salt

1 Melt the butter in a pan over a low heat. Add the onions and cook gently for 5 minutes.

2 Add the spinach and parsley and cook for a further 5 minutes.

3 Turn the mixture into a bowl and add the breadcrumbs, salt, Pernod and Tabasco.

4 Spread a thick layer of rock salt over the base of a large, shallow oven-proof dish and use it to bed in the oysters in their shells. Divide the spinach mixture evenly between the shells.

5 Bake in an oven preheated to 200°C/400°F/Gas Mark 6 for 10 minutes. Serve at once.

Poultry

RECIPES

1
CHICKEN MARYLAND

Succulent and savoury chicken portions served with corn fritters, fried bananas and bacon rolls.

2
STOVED CHICKEN

An easy and hearty recipe, cooked in a single pot.

3
CHICKEN WITH SAUSAGE AND RICE

Try to find spicy sausages to make this Mexican influenced dish.

4
FRIED CHICKEN

A classic dish with dozens of variations – use this as a starting point to develop your own recipe.

5
CHICKEN CHESAPEAKE

A typical American cookery style, combining meat with fish.

6
CAJUN CHICKEN

Make this spicy seasoning blend and use it to pep up your seafood, chops and steaks as well as chicken.

7
CHICKEN POT PIE

Chunks of cooked chicken in a creamy sauce, topped with fluffy mashed potato.

8
BAKED CHICKEN WITH LEMON

A tangy variation on chicken in breadcrumbs.

9
CHICKEN TETRAZZINI
A delicious pasta dish that provides an excellent way of using up leftover cooked chicken or turkey.

10
BUFFALO CHICKEN WINGS WITH BLUE CHEESE DIP
The heat level of this spicy dish can be adjusted to your personal taste.

11
BARBECUE CHICKEN
A tangy tomato barbecue sauce to bake on chicken so that you can enjoy the delicious flavour of barbecued chicken all year round.

12
CHICKEN FAJITAS
Floury tortillas filled with spicy chicken and served with peppers, salsa and soured cream.

13
CHICKEN WITH DUMPLINGS
A hearty casserole topped with soft dumplings for a substantial meal.

14
CHICKEN CREOLE
A colourful and flavoursome dish from the deep South of America.

CHICKEN MARYLAND

SERVES: 4
PREPARATION TIME: 35 MINUTES

45ml (3tbspn) plain flour
Salt and pepper
8 chicken thighs
1 egg, beaten
125g (4oz) fresh white breadcrumbs
25g (1oz) butter
60ml (4tbspn) vegetable oil
Corn fritters: see page 26
Fried bananas
Bacon rolls

1 Mix together the flour and seasoning. Roll the chicken pieces in the seasoned flour and dip in the beaten egg. Toss in the breadcrumbs until evenly coated.

2 Heat the butter and oil together in a large shallow pan over a medium to high heat. Add the chicken pieces and fry for 10 minutes, turning frequently, until evenly browned. Reduce the heat to low and cook for a further 20 minutes, turning occasionally.

3 Check the chicken is cooked by piercing the thickest part of the joint with a sharp knife. The juices should run clear.

4 Serve with sweetcorn fritters, chunks of peeled bananas fried in hot butter for 5 minutes, and streaky bacon rolled, secured with a skewer or cocktail stick, and grilled until crisp.

STOVED CHICKEN

This is a typical American country recipe where everything is cooked together in one pot.

SERVES: 4
PREPARATION TIME: 3 HOURS

25g (1oz) butter + extra for greasing
30ml (2tbspn) vegetable oil
4 chicken drumsticks
4 chicken thighs
150g (5oz) back bacon, chopped
900g (2lb) potatoes, peeled and sliced
2 onions, sliced
Salt and pepper
10ml (2tspn) fresh sage, chopped
570ml (1pt) chicken stock

1 Heat the butter and oil in a large pan over a medium heat. Add the chicken and bacon and cook, turning frequently, for 10 minutes, until golden brown.

2 Grease a large casserole dish generously with butter. Arrange half the potato slices over the base and cover with half the onion slices. Sprinkle with the sage.

3 Add the chicken and bacon and season. Cover with the remaining onion slices and top with the rest of the potato slices. Pour the stock over the top.

4 Cover and bake at 150°C/300°F/Gas Mark 2 for about 2 hours, until the chicken is tender and the potatoes are cooked. Cook for a further 20 minutes with the lid removed to crisp up the potatoes.

CHICKEN WITH SAUSAGE AND RICE

SERVES: 4
PREPARATION TIME: 1 HOUR 10 MINUTES

8 chicken drumsticks
15ml (1tbspn) vegetable oil
350g (12oz) chorizos or other spicy sausages, cut into 1cm (1/2 inch) slices
1 large onion, chopped
2 cloves garlic, crushed
1 green pepper, deseeded and chopped
1 green chilli, chopped
2 large tomatoes, peeled and chopped
30ml (2tbspn) fresh coriander, chopped
425ml (3/4pt) chicken stock
150g (5oz) long grain rice
110g (4oz) sweetcorn kernels
Salt and pepper
15ml (1tbspn) fresh parsley, chopped

1 Heat the oil in a large pan over a medium heat. Add the sausage and chicken and cook for about 20 minutes, turning frequently until the chicken skin is golden brown.

2 Remove the sausage and chicken from the pan, drain off all but 15ml (1tbspn) of the oil and add the onion, garlic, pepper and chilli. Fry for 5 minutes.

3 Add the tomatoes, coriander, chicken stock, rice and sweetcorn and bring to the boil.

4 Preheat the oven to 180°C/350°F/Gas Mark 4. Return the chicken and sausage to the pan and cover. Bake for 35–40 minutes, until the rice is tender and most of the moisture is absorbed. Season to taste and serve, sprinkled with parsley.

FRIED CHICKEN

SERVES: 4
PREPARATION TIME: 40 MINUTES

1 egg
150ml (1/4pt) milk
225g (8oz) plain flour
5ml (1tspn) salt
5ml (1tspn) ground white pepper
2.5ml (1/2tspn) dried thyme
2.5ml (1/2tspn) paprika
Pinch of cayenne pepper
Pinch of ground bay
2 skin-on chicken breasts, cut in half
4 skin-on chicken drumsticks
4 skin-on chicken thighs
Vegetable oil for frying

1 Whisk together the egg and milk.

2 Sieve together the flour, salt, pepper, thyme, paprika, cayenne and bay on to a large plate.

3 Dip the chicken into the milk and egg mix and then toss in the seasoned flour to coat well.

4 Heat about 150ml (1/4pt) of oil in a large pan over a medium heat. Add the chicken pieces and fry for about 10 minutes, turning occasionally.

5 Transfer the fried chicken pieces to a rack set over a baking tray and cook at 220°C/425°F/Gas Mark 7 for 20–25 minutes, until the portions are crisp and cooked through. Drain the portions on kitchen paper and serve at once.

CHICKEN CHESAPEAKE

SERVES: 4
PREPARATION TIME: 1HOUR 10 MINUTES

STUFFING
25g (1oz) butter
1 large onion, finely chopped
3 eating apples, peeled, cored and finely diced
Salt and pepper
45ml (3tbspn) brandy
400g (14oz) crab meat
4 large, skinless chicken breast fillets
2 eggs, beaten
Plain flour

1 First make the stuffing. Heat the butter in a pan over a medium heat. Add the onion and apple and cook for 10 minutes, stirring occasionally. Add the salt, pepper and brandy. Bring to the boil and simmer for 10 minutes, or until the brandy has evaporated and the mix looks dry.

2 Transfer the mix to a bowl, cool and then mix in the crab meat.

3 Place the chicken fillets, one at a time, between two layers of cling film. Pound the fillets with a steak hammer or rolling pin until about double their original surface area.

4 Divide the crab mixture evenly into four and spread over the chicken fillets. Roll up the fillets and secure with a cocktail stick. Dip in the egg and toss in the flour.

5 Arrange the fillets in a lightly greased, shallow oven-proof dish and bake at 180°C/350°F/Gas Mark 4 for 30 minutes. Remember to remove the cocktail sticks before serving.

CAJUN CHICKEN

The term Cajun usually refers to food that has been dusted in a spicy coating before cooking. The basic seasoning can be used on steaks, chops, fish or prawns as well as the chicken suggested in this recipe.

SERVES: 4
PREPARATION TIME: 20 MINUTES + STANDING TIME

4 large, skin-on chicken fillets

SEASONING
25g (1oz) salt
25g (1oz) garlic salt
50g (2oz) white pepper
50g (2oz) black pepper
75g (3oz) cayenne pepper
50g (2oz) dried oregano
25g (1oz) mustard powder
50g (2oz) dried basil
25g (1oz) ground coriander
25g (1oz) ground cumin

1 Blend all the seasoning ingredients together. This mix can be made in advance and stored in an airtight container, such as a screw-topped jar, until ready for use.

2 Dust the chicken with the seasoning and leave for 30 minutes. This gives the flavours a chance to start penetrating the meat.

3 Cook under a medium grill for about 15 minutes, turning once.

CHICKEN POT PIE

SERVES: 4
PREPARATION TIME: 1 HOUR

700g (1½lb) potatoes, peeled
50g (2oz) butter
1 onion, finely chopped
1 clove garlic, crushed
110g (4oz) mushrooms, sliced
25g (1oz) plain flour
275ml (½pt) full cream milk
150ml (¼pt) double cream
110g (4oz) frozen peas
Salt and pepper
450g (1lb) cooked chicken, cut into 1cm (½ inch) cubes
25g (1oz) butter
Milk

1 Boil the potatoes in salted water until tender.

2 Meanwhile, heat the butter in a pan over a medium heat. Add the onion and garlic and cook for 5 minutes. Add the mushrooms and cook for a further 5 minutes. Stir in the flour and cook for a further 5 minutes.

3 Remove the pan from the heat and gradually mix in the milk and cream, stirring vigorously to prevent lumps. Add the peas and simmer the sauce for 5 minutes. Season to taste.

4 Stir the chicken into the sauce and pour into a shallow, oven-proof dish.

5 Mash the potatoes with the remaining butter and enough milk to make a creamy purée. Season to taste. Spread the potato over the chicken mixture and mark into a pattern with the prongs of a fork.

6 Bake in an oven preheated to 180°C/350°F/Gas Mark 4 for 30–40 minutes until the potato is browned and the chicken is piping hot.

BAKED CHICKEN WITH LEMON

SERVES: 4
PREPARATION TIME: 35 MINUTES

50g (2oz) fresh white breadcrumbs
25g (1oz) parmesan cheese, grated
30ml (2tbspn) parsley, finely chopped
Grated zest of 1 lemon
4 breast fillets, skinless
40g (1½oz) butter, melted

SAUCE
50g (2oz) butter
1 clove garlic, crushed
Juice of 1 lemon
Salt
Freshly ground black pepper

1 Mix the breadcrumbs, cheese, parsley and lemon zest.

2 Dip the top of the fillets into the melted butter and press into the breadcrumb mixture. Arrange the fillets, breadcrumb side up, in a lightly greased oven-proof dish.

3 Bake the fillets at 190°C/375°F/Gas Mark 5 for about 25 minutes.

4 Meanwhile, make the sauce. Heat the butter in a small pan over a medium heat. Add the garlic and cook for 5 minutes. Stir in the lemon juice.

5 Pour the sauce over the breast fillets and cook for a further 5 minutes. Serve at once.

CHICKEN TETRAZZINI

This dish was reputedly created to honour an Italian opera singer. It is an excellent way of using up leftover cooked chicken or turkey.

SERVES: 4
PREPARATION TIME: 1 HOUR

225g (8oz) spaghetti
50g (2oz) butter
225g (8oz) button mushrooms, sliced
30ml (2tbspn) plain flour
425ml (3/4pt) chicken stock
275ml (1/2pt) double cream
45ml (3tbspn) dry sherry
Salt and pepper
350g (12oz) cooked chicken or turkey, roughly diced
50g (2oz) parmesan cheese, grated

1 Cook the spaghetti in plenty of boiling salted water until just tender. Drain and rinse in cold water.

2 Meanwhile melt the butter in a large pan over a medium heat. Add the mushrooms and cook for about 10 minutes, until browned. Stir in the flour and cook for 2 minutes.

3 Slowly add the stock, stirring briskly, and bring to the boil.

4 Add the cream and sherry and simmer for 5 minutes. Season.

5 Place the spaghetti in the bottom of a greased, oven-proof dish. Top with half the sauce, then cover with the chicken or turkey. Pour over the remaining sauce and sprinkle with the parmesan.

6 Bake at 180°C/350°F/Gas Mark 4 for about 30 minutes, until heated through and golden brown.

BUFFALO CHICKEN WINGS WITH BLUE CHEESE DIP

There are restaurants in America that serve nothing but buffalo wings, with different degrees of heat. Mild, warm, hot and radioactive is one heat-grading used. Adjust the heat to your taste by varying the levels of cayenne and chilli. Remember that the blue cheese dip cools the heat down a bit, so live dangerously!

SERVES: 4–6
PREPARATION TIME: 30 MINUTES + MARINATION TIME

3 cloves garlic, crushed
15ml (1tbspn) cayenne pepper
15ml (1tbspn) chilli powder
Juice of 1 lemon
30ml (2tbspn) paprika
60ml (4tbspn) olive oil
15ml (1tbspn) tomato purée
1.5kg (3lbs) chicken wings

1 Make a paste with the garlic, cayenne, chilli, lemon juice and paprika. Gradually mix in the olive oil and tomato purée.

2 In a large glass or china bowl, tumble the wings in the spicy paste until they are evenly coated. Cover the bowl with cling film and refrigerate for at least 4 hours, or overnight if preferred.

3 Tumble the wings again to ensure an even coating.

4 Preheat the oven to 220°C/425°F/Gas Mark 7. Arrange the wings on a baking tray lined with aluminium foil and bake for 20–25 minutes, until crisp.

5 Serve the wings with blue cheese dip on the next page.

BLUE CHEESE DIP

MAKES: 570ML (1PT)
PREPARATION TIME: 10 MINUTES

175g (6oz) blue cheese – Danish blue works well
1 small onion, finely chopped
2 cloves garlic, crushed
215ml (7.5 fl oz) mayonnaise
150ml (¼pt) soured cream
30ml (2tbspn) lemon juice
30ml (2tbspn) fresh parsley, chopped

1 Place the blue cheese in a bowl and mash with a fork.

2 Add the remaining ingredients and mix thoroughly. You can make a completely smooth paste or retain some texture if you prefer.

3 Turn the dip into one large dish or individual serving dishes and sprinkle with chopped parsley.

BARBECUE CHICKEN

You will find hundreds of variations on barbecue sauces – in fact, there are several different ones in this book. They can be sharp, sweet, smoky, tomatoey or even a combination of all of these, and obviously you can experiment with a number of recipes to find your favourite.

SERVES: 4
PREPARATION TIME: About 40 minutes

About 900g (2lb) skin-on chicken joints – drumsticks, thighs and wings

BARBECUE SAUCE
1 large onion, very finely chopped
275ml (1/2pt) tomato ketchup
50g (2oz) made mustard, preferably American style
2 cloves garlic, crushed
45ml (3tbspn) Worcestershire sauce
45ml (3tbspn) red wine or cider vinegar
15ml (1tbspn) soy sauce
15ml (1tbspn) soft brown sugar
Tabasco sauce

1 To make the sauce, simply combine all the ingredients, adding Tabasco to taste. If you would like a smoother sauce, simply whiz it in a blender at this point.

2 Brush the sauce over the chicken portions and either bake, grill or barbecue them until tender and cooked. The juices should run clear when the thickest part of the joint is pierced with a sharp knife or skewer. Brush with more sauce at least once during the cooking time.

CHICKEN FAJITAS

SERVES: 4
PREPARATION TIME: 45 MINUTES

2 chicken breast fillets
Cajun seasoning – see page 87
Oil for frying
1 red pepper, deseeded and sliced
1 green pepper, deseeded and sliced
Soured cream
Tomato salsa – see page 26

TORTILLAS
450g (1lb) plain flour
5ml (1tspn) baking powder
5ml (1tspn) salt
22.5ml (1½tbspn) vegetable oil
175ml (6fl oz) cold water

1 First make the tortillas. Sift the flour, baking powder and salt into a bowl. Make a well in the centre and add the oil and as much water as is required to make a stiff dough. Knead until smooth. Divide the dough into 12 equally sized pieces and roll each into a ball.

2 On a well floured surface, roll out each ball into a thin circle about 15cm (6 inches) across. You may find it easier to roll the dough between two sheets of baking parchment, but don't worry if you don't achieve perfect circles.

3 Heat a heavy based frying pan over a medium to high heat. Grease very lightly. Cook the tortillas, one or two at a time, depending on the size of your pan, for about 45 seconds on each side. Keep warm wrapped in tea towels or foil. Do not allow them to dry out or they will crumble when you try to roll them.

4 Meanwhile, dust the fillets with seasoning and cook under a preheated medium to high grill for about 15 minutes, turning once. Cut into thin strips and keep warm.

5 Heat 15ml (1tbspn) vegetable oil in a pan over a high heat. Quickly fry the pepper slices for about 5 minutes.

6 To serve the fajitas, take a tortilla and top with the chicken and pepper strips. Add a spoonful of soured cream and salsa to taste. Turn in the ends and roll up. Eat with your fingers. It is good fun, for a casual supper, to supply all the prepared ingredients and let your guests roll their own fajitas.

CHICKEN WITH DUMPLINGS

SERVES: 4
PREPARATION TIME: 1 HOUR 15 MINUTES

60ml (4tbspn) vegetable oil
4 large chicken joints
1 small onion, finely chopped
150ml (1/4pt) dry white wine
570ml (1pt) chicken stock
2 stalks celery, finely sliced
1 small red pepper, deseeded and sliced
1 leek, cleaned and thinly sliced
Salt and pepper
Pinch of nutmeg
225g (8oz) plain flour
10ml (2tspn) baking powder
50g (2oz) butter, softened
About 150ml (1/4pt) full cream milk
15ml (1tbspn) cornflour

1 Heat the oil in a large pan over a medium heat. Add the chicken pieces and fry, turning, until well browned all over. Remove from the pan.

2 Add the onion to the pan and cook for 1 minute. Stir in the wine and bring to the boil. Simmer for 1 minute.

3 Return the chicken to the pan with the stock, celery, pepper and leek. Add a pinch of salt, pepper and nutmeg and bring to the boil. Simmer for 30–40 minutes, until the chicken juices run clear when the thickest part of the joint is pierced with a sharp knife.

4 Meanwhile sift the flour, baking powder, and some salt and pepper into a bowl. Rub in the butter until the mixture resembles fine breadcrumbs and then add enough milk to make a soft dough.

5 Gently knead the mix together and roll out on a lightly floured work surface to 1cm (1/2 inch) thick. Cut into circles 5cm (2 inches) in diameter.

6 When the chicken is cooked, lift it out of the stock and keep it warm in a low oven.

7 Mix the cornflour with enough water to make a thin paste and add to the stock, stirring briskly. Bring to the boil. Sit the dumplings on top of the stock and simmer, covered, for 18–20 minutes, until the dumplings are well risen and firm.

8 To serve, lift the dumplings out of the sauce using a slotted spoon and arrange over the chicken. Pour the sauce over the chicken and dumplings and serve at once.

CHICKEN CREOLE

SERVES: 4
PREPARATION TIME: 1 HOUR 10 MINUTES

15ml (1tbspn) olive oil
2 onions, chopped
2 cloves garlic, chopped
1 green pepper, deseeded and chopped
3 stalks celery, chopped
425g (15½oz) can chopped tomatoes in juice
2 bay leaves
10ml (2tspn) paprika
2.5ml (½tspn) cayenne pepper
Pinch dried thyme
Salt
700g (1½lb) skinless breast fillets, cut into strips

1 Heat the oil in a large pan over a medium heat. Add the onion, garlic, pepper and celery and cook, stirring occasionally, for 10 minutes.

2 Add the tomatoes, bay leaves, paprika, cayenne and thyme and bring to the boil. Simmer gently for 30 minutes.

3 Add the chicken and simmer for about 25 minutes, until it is thoroughly cooked. Season to taste.

4 Remove the bay leaves and serve on a bed of rice.

Meat and Game

RECIPES

1

FILLET MIGNON

A classic recipe for cooking America's most popular meat.

2

BEEF BURRITOS

A spicy beef parcel, wrapped in a flour tortilla. Deep fry them to create beef chimichangas.

3

LOUISIANA BEEF CASSEROLE

A colourful casserole successfully blending a number of unusual ingredients.

4

RABBIT STEW

A rich and hearty casserole.

5

MEATLOAF

One basic recipe and several variations on this dish, which is now something of an American institution. A real family favourite, you can adapt it to your own tastes.

6

STUFFED PEPPERS

A classic, Southern-style recipe, which once again lends itself to adaptation.

7

MEATBALLS WITH TOMATO SAUCE

Little minced beef meatballs, flavoured with herbs, in a rich tomato sauce.

8

COWBOY HASH

A delicious recipe, somewhat adapted from its basic beginnings.

9

CORN DUMPLING CASSEROLE

A rich beef casserole flavoured with peppers and tomatoes and topped with light and fluffy sweetcorn dumplings.

10

BARBECUE RIBS

Another classic, and another recipe ripe for adaptation. Everybody has their own idea of what a barbecue sauce should be, so use your own recipe if you prefer.

11

NEW ENGLAND BOILED DINNER

A traditional example of American-style one-pot cookery.

12

BAKED HAM

A glazed gammon joint given extra punch with bourbon.

13

VENISON PIE

A rich venison casserole, flavoured with red wine, under a puff pastry crust.

Steaks

America is justly famous for its steaks, coming in all shapes and sizes, large, huge and obscene! Some restaurants offer 2kg (64oz) steaks. It should be remembered, however, that America is also the nation of the "doggy bag". If a diner leaves a proportion of his meal, he is regularly asked if he would like to take the remains home. Bearing in mind that these leftovers could be 450g (1lb) of finest steak, it's easy to see why this custom is supported by diners.

Steaks tend to be served quite plainly, usually cooked on a griddle to retain succulence and give a faint char-grilled flavour. The steaks most likely to be served are fillet, sirloin, rib eye and T-bone. Obviously such huge steaks are more rare outside America and big is not necessarily beautiful. Since steak tends to be something of a treat, why not indulge in a piece of Aberdeen Angus, a rich, red meat marbled with fat and full of flavour?

COOK'S TIP

A delicious variation is to place folded burritos in an ovenproof dish, sprinkle thickly with grated cheddar, and flash under a hot grill to melt the cheese.

To turn these into beef chimichangas, secure the fold of the filled tortilla with a cocktail stick. Heat vegetable oil in a deep-fat fryer or a deep, heavy based saucepan. Fry the chimichangas for about 5 minutes, until crisp and golden. Drain well on kitchen paper and serve at once.

It is possible to buy ready made tortillas, making this a very quick dish to prepare. Be sure to buy the flour rather than corn tortillas.

LOUISIANA BEEF CASSEROLE

Some of the ingredients in this colourful casserole may look rather unusual, but the flavours work beautifully together.

SERVES: 6
PREPARATION TIME: 3 HOURS 15 MINUTES

30ml (2tbspn) vegetable oil
1 large onion, chopped
3 cloves garlic, crushed
900g (2lb) stewing beef, cut into 2cm (3/4 inch) cubes
30ml (2tbspn) plain flour
420g (14 1/2 oz) can chopped tomatoes in juice
570ml (1pt) beef stock
5ml (1tspn) dried thyme
Pinch ground bay leaf
450g (1lb) pumpkin, cut into 2cm (3/4 inch) cubes
4 potatoes, peeled and cut into 2cm (3/4 inch) cubes
110g (4oz) baby sweetcorn
420g (14 1/2 oz) can peach slices in natural juice

1 Heat the oil in a large, oven-proof casserole over a medium heat. Add the onion and garlic and fry gently for 10 minutes.

2 Toss the meat in the flour and add to the pan. Cook for about 10 minutes, turning frequently until the beef is browned all over.

3 Add the tomatoes, stock, thyme and bay leaf and bring to the boil. Cover and transfer to an oven preheated to 180°C/350°F/Gas Mark 4 and cook for 2 hours.

4 Remove from the oven and add the pumpkin, potatoes, baby corn and the peaches with their juice. Cover and cook for a further 30–40 minutes, until the vegetables are tender.

RABBIT STEW

In the hunting-shooting-fishing states, rabbit is a popular meat and this recipe, which involves a long, slow cooking, shows it off at its best. Most large supermarkets now stock a range of rabbit joints, both fresh and frozen.

SERVES: 4
PREPARATION TIME: 3 HOURS

30ml (2tbspn) vegetable oil
4 plump rabbit joints
1 large onion, chopped
3 cloves garlic, crushed
3 sticks celery, chopped
2 carrots, sliced
1 small green pepper, deseeded and sliced
10ml (2tspn) salt
5ml (1tspn) black pepper
30ml (2tbspn) tomato purée
5ml (1tspn) dried thyme
275ml ($^1/_2$pt) beef stock

1 Heat the oil in a large, oven-proof casserole over a medium heat. Add the rabbit pieces and brown on all sides. Remove the rabbit from the pan and add the onion, garlic, celery, carrots and pepper and fry for about 10 minutes, until the vegetables are beginning to soften.

2 Return the rabbit joints to the pan. Add the seasoning, tomato purée, thyme and stock, and cover. Transfer to an oven preheated to 180°C/350°F/Gas Mark 4 for 2–2$^1/_2$ hours, until the meat is tender.

3 Serve with creamed potatoes and green vegetables.

MEATLOAF

A popular American meal for the whole family, this recipe could not be easier to make. It can be adapted in an almost infinite number of ways – there are some suggestions below.

SERVES: 4
PREPARATION TIME: 1 HOUR 20 MINUTES

450g (1lb) minced beef
110g (4oz) mushrooms, finely chopped
50g (2oz) fresh white breadcrumbs
110g (4oz) streaky bacon, finely chopped
1 small onion, finely chopped
1 clove garlic, crushed
5ml (1tspn) dried thyme
60ml (4tbspn) tomato ketchup
1 egg, beaten
Salt and pepper

1 In a bowl, mix the beef, mushrooms, breadcrumbs, bacon, onion, garlic, thyme, tomato ketchup and egg until thoroughly blended. Season well with salt and pepper.

2 Spoon the mixture into a greased 900g (2lb) loaf tin and press down gently.

3 Bake in a preheated oven 180°C/350°F/Gas Mark 4 for 1 hour 15 minutes. Turn out carefully and serve.

Variations

After an hour's cooking, turn the loaf out on to a baking tray. Smear it all over with ready made mild mustard and return it to the oven for 15 minutes.

Place half the meat mixture in the tin, cover with 110g (4oz) of crumbled blue cheese and top with the remaining meat mixture. Bake as above.

Slice a green pepper and arrange the slices in the base of the tin. Cover with the meat mixture and bake as above.

STUFFED PEPPERS

A classic Southern-style recipe that can be made with almost any cold meat and vegetables you have to hand.

SERVES: 6
PREPARATION TIME: 50 MINUTES

6 green peppers – about 110g (4oz) each
15ml (1tbspn) vegetable oil
1 small onion, chopped
2 stalks celery, finely chopped
2 tomatoes, peeled and chopped
175g (6oz) cooked long-grain rice
275g (10oz) cooked meat (ham, chicken, beef, sausages), chopped
1 egg
Salt and pepper
420g (14½oz) can chopped tomatoes in juice
150ml (¼pt) stock– use a flavour to complement your choice of meat

1 Cut the stalk ends off the peppers and retain for use as a lid. Carefully scoop out and discard the seeds and membranes, keeping the peppers whole.

2 Bring a large saucepan of water to the boil, add the peppers, cover and simmer for 2 minutes. Drain the peppers and stand them upright, with the opening at the top, in a fairly deep oven-proof dish.

3 Heat the oil in a small pan over a medium heat. Add the onion and cook gently until softened.

4 Mix the onion with the celery, fresh tomatoes, rice and meat and mix in the egg. Season with salt and pepper and pack into the peppers. Top with the reserved lids, set at an angle.

5 Mix together the tinned tomatoes, stock and seasoning and pour over and around the peppers.

6 Place the dish in an oven preheated to 190°C/375°F/Gas Mark 5 for 30–35 minutes.

MEATBALLS WITH TOMATO SAUCE

SERVES: 4
PREPARATION TIME: 1 HOUR

MEATBALLS
700g (1½lb) lean minced beef
110g (4oz) fresh white breadcrumbs
1 clove garlic, crushed
1 small onion, very finely chopped
2 eggs, beaten
15ml (1tbspn) chopped parsley
5ml (1tspn) chopped thyme

2 Place all the marinade ingredients in a pan and bring to the boil, stirring well to ensure they are evenly mixed. Pour over the ribs.

3 Return the tray to the oven and cook for about 45 minutes, basting every 10–15 minutes. Serve hot.

These ribs can be cooked over a barbecue. Precook as in stage 1 and coat with marinade. Then transfer the ribs to the barbecue and continue cooking, turning frequently and basting with spare marinade, until tender.

You will find it saves on washing up if you line the baking tray with foil prior to cooking the ribs.

NEW ENGLAND BOILED DINNER

A traditional family dish, cooked in one pot. Reserve the cooking stock, as it makes an excellent base for soups

SERVES: 4
PREPARATION TIME: 2 HOURS 15 MINUTES

900g (2lb) salt beef joint
2 large onions, cut into quarters
4 potatoes, cut into large chunks
2 small turnips, cut into quarters
4 large carrots, cut into thick slices
1 small cabbage, cut into quarters

1 Place the beef in a large saucepan and cover with water. Cover the pan and bring to the boil. Reduce to a simmer and cook for 1½ hours. Skim and discard any scum that appears during cooking.

2 Add the root vegetables and simmer for a further 25–30 minutes.

3 Add the cabbage to the pan and cook for a further 10–15 minutes, until the cabbage is tender.

4 Remove the meat from the pan to a large serving dish and arrange the vegetables around the joint.

BAKED HAM

SERVES: 8

PREPARATION TIME: 2 HOURS 45 MINUTES + SOAKING TIME

1.8kg (4lb) smoked gammon joint
275ml (1/2pt) whisky, preferably bourbon
110g (4oz) black treacle
30ml (2tbspn) strong made-up mustard

1 Place the gammon in a large bowl, cover with cold water and leave to soak overnight.

2 Drain the gammon and place in the centre of a large piece of foil, big enough to wrap it, spread over a baking tray.

3 Mix the whisky, treacle and mustard together and spread over the gammon. Wrap the foil around the meat, trying not to let it touch the glaze, and pinch the ends to make a sealed parcel.

4 Bake the gammon in an oven preheated to 190°C/375°F/Gas Mark 5 for 1½ hours. Carefully remove from the oven and open the foil. With a sharp knife peel back the rind and discard. Score the revealed fat into squares and baste well with the glaze.

5 Return the gammon to the oven, with the foil still open, and cook for a further 30–40 minutes, basting frequently, until the glaze is crisp and dark.

6 Serve hot or cold.

VENISON PIE

Venison is probably the most popular game in America and has been for centuries. Early colonists soon learnt from the native Americans that venison was a plentiful source of meat.

SERVES: 6

PREPARATION TIME: 3 HOURS 30 MINUTES + MARINATION TIME

275ml (1/2pt) red wine
1 onion, finely chopped
2 bay leaves
6 black peppercorns
1.5kg (3lb) boneless venison, cut into 2.5cm (1 inch) cubes
60ml (4tbspn) vegetable oil
30ml (2tbspn) plain flour
1 stick celery, sliced
2 carrots, sliced
225g (8oz) mushrooms, sliced
275ml (1/2pt) beef stock
Salt and pepper
225g (8oz) ready made puff pastry, defrosted if frozen
Beaten egg or milk for glazing

1 Mix together the wine, onion, bay leaves and pepper and pour over the venison in a large bowl. Cover and refrigerate overnight.

2 Drain the meat, reserving the marinade, and pat dry on kitchen paper.

3 Heat the oil in a large pan over a medium to high heat. Toss the venison in the flour and fry it, in batches if necessary, until browned all over. Transfer to a casserole. Add the celery, carrots and mushrooms to the pan and fry for 2–3 minutes. Transfer to the casserole.

4 Sieve the marinade, discarding the solids, into the pan and bring to the boil. Scrape down the pan well. Simmer for 15 minutes, then add to the casserole with the stock.

5 Cover the casserole and cook in an oven preheated to 160°C/325°F/Gas Mark 3 for 2–2½ hours, until the meat is tender. Season to taste and transfer to a pie dish. Increase the oven temperature to 220°C/425°F/Gas Mark 7.

6 Roll out the pastry and cut a strip to cover the lip of the pie dish. Moisten the lip with water and cover with the strip of pastry. Moisten this strip and cover the whole pie with the remaining pastry. Seal and crimp the edges. Make leaves from the pastry offcuts and decorate the pie. Glaze all over with egg or milk and cut a slit in the top of the pastry to act as a vent.

7 Bake the pie for 25–30 minutes, until the pastry is golden and well risen.

Vegetables and Salads

RECIPES

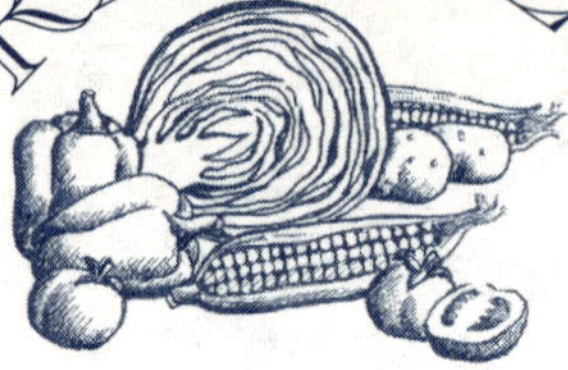

1
BOSTON BAKED BEANS

It is worthwhile trying the real thing at least once. It may not be as convenient as opening a tin, but the flavour should be experienced.

2
REFRIED BEANS

A delicious accompaniment to Southern-style dishes.

3
HOPPIN' JOHN

A hearty side dish, based on black eyed peas and rice.

4
SUCCOTASH

Probably deriving from America's earliest inhabitants, this simple side dish combines sweetcorn and butter beans.

5
HASH BROWNS

Forget the little frozen cakes sold here as hash browns. In America they are crisply browned cakes of grated potato, which retain their loose texture.

6
POTATO SALAD

A classic American accompaniment. Use this basic recipe to develop your own individual version.

7
COURGETTE CASSEROLE
An excellent recipe for using up a glut of courgettes, this is good enough to serve as a light supper or lunch dish.

8
COLESLAW
Another classic recipe open to adaptation, with any number of possible variations.

9
WALDORF SALAD
A refreshing combination of celery and apples with the crunch of walnuts, bound in mayonnaise.

10
TWICE-BAKED POTATOES
Baked potatoes, with the filling scooped out and mashed with seasonings before being piled back into the skins and reheated.

11
CAESAR'S SALAD
A delicious salad, made even more crunchy by the inclusion of croutons.

12
PARSNIP GRATIN
Creamy parsnips topped with crispy breadcrumbs and baked.

BOSTON BAKED BEANS

This must be one of the most famous American dishes. As the beans need a long, slow cooking, you may find it more economical to double the recipe and freeze half for a later date.

SERVES: 6

PREPARATION TIME: 2 HOURS 15MINUTES + SOAKING TIME

450g (1lb) haricot beans
30ml (2tbspn) dark brown sugar
30ml (2tbspn) black treacle
45ml (3tbspn) Worcestershire sauce
15ml (1tbspn) mustard powder
425ml (3/4pt) water
1 large onion, chopped
4 belly of pork slices
Salt and pepper

1 Soak the beans in cold water overnight. Drain.

2 Mix together the sugar, treacle, Worcestershire sauce, mustard powder and water.

3 Place the beans and onion in a large oven-proof pot with a well fitting lid. Pour the water mixture over the beans and top with the belly of pork slices. Cover with the lid.

4 Cook in an oven preheated to 150°C/300°F/Gas Mark 2 for 2 hours. Stir and add more water if the beans begin to look dry. reduce the heat to 140°C/275°F/Gas Mark 1 and cook for a further 1½–2 hours until the beans are tender.

5 Cut the pork slices into chunks and stir into the beans. Add salt and pepper to taste and serve.

REFRIED BEANS

This is a classic accompaniment to Southern-style foods, particularly tortillas and burritos.

SERVES: 4–6
PREPARATION TIME: 1 HOUR 45 MINUTES + SOAKING TIME

225g (8oz) pinto beans
1 large onion, finely chopped
3–4 cloves garlic, crushed
5–10ml (1–2tspn) chilli powder
10ml (2tspn) salt
Pinch of black pepper
Pinch of powdered bay leaf
30ml (2tbspn) vegetable oil

1 Soak the beans in cold water overnight. Drain and place in a large saucepan. Cover with fresh cold water, bring to the boil and simmer gently for 50–60 minutes, until the beans are tender.

2 Add the onion to the beans with the garlic, chilli powder, salt, pepper and bay leaf and cook for a further 20–30 minutes, until the beans are very soft.

3 Drain the bean mixture and mash thoroughly, adjusting the seasoning to taste.

4 Heat the oil in a large frying pan over a medium heat. Add the bean mixture and press down well. Cook for 15 minutes, turning from time to time. The mixture should begin to look drier. Serve piping hot.

HOPPIN' JOHN

This is a hearty side dish, which probably originated in the rice plantations of the deep South. It is good served with spicy sausages or chops. Black-eyed peas are confusingly actually beans – small and cream coloured with a black spot.

SERVES: 4–6
PREPARATION TIME: 45 MINUTES + SOAKING TIME

225g (8oz) black-eyed peas
75g (3oz) smoked streaky bacon, chopped
1 onion, chopped
3 cloves garlic, crushed
Pinch of cayenne pepper
Pinch of dried thyme
Pinch of ground bay
Salt and pepper
110g (4oz) long-grain rice

1 Cover the beans in cold water and soak overnight. Drain and place in a large pan, covering with fresh cold water. Bring to the boil and simmer for 30 minutes, until the beans are tender.

2 Fry the bacon in a pan over a high heat until crisp. Remove, and fry the onion and garlic in the bacon fat for 10 minutes, until beginning to colour and soften.

3 Add the bacon, onion, garlic, seasoning and rice to the peas. Cover and cook gently for 15 minutes, until the rice is cooked. Check the liquid level during this time – there needs to be enough liquid to cook the rice, so add more water if necessary, but the finished dish should be quite dry. Serve piping hot.

SUCCOTASH

This side dish, which probably derived from native American cooking, is particularly delicious made with fresh sweetcorn.

SERVES 4–6
PREPARATION TIME: 10 MINUTES

2 x 350g (12oz) cans sweetcorn kernels, drained
200g (7oz) can butter beans, drained
25g (1oz) butter
Pinch of salt
Pinch of pepper
2.5ml (½tspn) paprika
45ml (3tbspn) soured cream
Fresh parsley, chopped

1 Place the sweetcorn and butter beans in a pan over a medium heat with the butter, salt, pepper and paprika. Heat through gently, stirring as the butter melts.

2 Stir in the soured cream and heat through gently. Adjust the seasoning to taste and sprinkle with chopped parsley to serve.

If you are lucky enough to have fresh corn on the cob, use this. Slice the kernels off the cob using a sharp knife. Cook them in boiling, lightly salted water for 10–15 minutes, until just tender. Drain and proceed as above. You can also replace the butter beans with lightly cooked fresh broad beans if you wish.

HASH BROWNS

This famous American dish is often served for breakfast and is excellent with crisply grilled bacon and fried or scrambled eggs, but hash browns are also good served with sausages or fish fingers for supper.

SERVES: 4

PREPARATION TIME: 25 MINUTES

700g (1½lb) potatoes, coarsely grated
1 large onion, thinly sliced
2 cloves garlic, crushed
5ml (1tspn) salt
5ml (1tspn) black pepper
45ml (3tbspn) vegetable oil

1 Place the potatoes in a pan, cover with cold water and bring to the boil. Drain immediately and rinse under cold water. Pat dry in a tea towel.

2 Place the potato, onion, garlic, salt and pepper in a bowl and mix together. Add 30ml (2tbspn) oil and mix well.

3 Heat a large, heavy based frying pan over a medium to high heat and add the potato mixture. Fry for about 15 minutes, pressing down and turning frequently, so the potato begins to brown and becomes crisp. Add the remaining oil if necessary.

4 Check that the potato is cooked through and is as brown and crispy as you wish. Serve piping hot.

POTATO SALAD

SERVES: 4

PREPARATION TIME: 30 MINUTES + CHILLING TIME

700g (1½lb) new potatoes, washed but not peeled
1 hard boiled egg, chopped
6 spring onions, chopped
30ml (2tbspn) olive oil
15ml (1tbspn) white wine vinegar
Pinch of mustard powder
15ml (1tbspn) mild made-up mustard
5ml (1tspn) salt
1 stalk celery, chopped
1 gherkin, finely chopped
200g (7oz) mayonnaise
Paprika
Fresh parsley, chopped

1 Boil the potatoes until just tender. Drain and cool until you can just handle them. Then cut into evenly sized chunks, about 2cm (¾ inch) square.

2 Place warm potato pieces in a bowl with the hard boiled egg and spring onions.

3 Blend the oil and vinegar with the mustard powder and pour it on to the potato mix. Toss gently until the vinaigrette is absorbed. Cover and refrigerate until cold – about an hour.

4 Mix the made-up mustard, salt, celery and gherkin into the mayonnaise and blend with the potato mix. Pile into a serving dish and chill until required. Garnish with paprika and parsley before serving.

COURGETTE CASSEROLE

SERVES: 6
PREPARATION TIME: 1 HOUR 15 MINUTES + STANDING TIME

6 courgettes, coarsely grated
10ml (2tspn) salt
110g (4oz) cheddar cheese, grated
1 small onion, finely sliced
4 slices bread, crusts removed and crumbled into coarse crumbs
2 eggs, beaten
Pinch of black pepper

1 Place the courgettes in a bowl and sprinkle with the salt. Allow them to stand for one hour and then rinse with water through a sieve. The salt pulls some of the moisture out of the courgettes. Shake well and pat dry with kitchen paper.

2 In a large bowl, mix the courgettes, cheese, onion and breadcrumbs. Add the eggs and pepper and mix well.

3 Grease an oven-proof dish and turn the mixture into this. Don't worry that it looks quite sloppy at this stage. Smooth the top and bake at 180°C/350°F/Gas Mark 4 for about an hour, until well risen and firm.

COLESLAW

SERVES: 6
PREPARATION TIME: 20 MINUTES

1 small, hard white cabbage, about 450–700g (1–1½lb)
2 onions
4 carrots
About 275ml (½pt) mayonnaise
15ml (1tbspn) mild mustard

1 Quarter the cabbage, remove the outside leaves and the stalk and shred into very fine strips. Peel and quarter the onions and shred very finely. Peel the carrots and grate coarsely.

2 Blend the mayonnaise and mustard.

3 In a large bowl, mix together the prepared vegetables. Bind together with the mayonnaise mix, adding as much as you wish.

4 Turn into a serving dish, cover and chill until required.

Variations

Add a handful of raisins and flaked almonds to the mix.

Add a shredded green pepper and two stalks of finely diced celery to the mix. Sprinkle with sesame seeds just before serving.

Make with very finely shredded red cabbage instead of white.

Add peeled and segmented mandarin oranges, halved and deseeded green grapes, and fresh or canned pineapple chunks to the mix.

Instead of mayonnaise, use crème fraîche or fromage frais.

WALDORF SALAD

SERVES: 4
PREPARATION TIME: 15 MINUTES

2 crisp red-skinned eating apples
2 crisp green-skinned eating apples
15ml (1tbspn) lemon juice
3 stalks celery
75g (3oz) walnut pieces
150ml (1/4pt) mayonnaise
Lettuce leaves

1 Core the apples and cut into 1cm (1/2 inch) cubes. Place in a bowl and toss in lemon juice to prevent the cut edges going brown.

2 Cut the celery stalks into thick slices and chop the walnuts roughly.

3 Add the celery and walnuts to the apples and mix. Add the mayonnaise and toss together lightly until all the ingredients are evenly blended. Cover and chill until required.

4 Shred the lettuce leaves and use to cover a serving plate. Pile the apple mixture on top.

As with most salads, this is best made only shortly before it is served. If kept too long, the apples, celery and walnuts will begin to lose their crisp textures.

TWICE-BAKED POTATOES

SERVES: 4
PREPARATION TIME: 1 HOUR 50 MINUTES

4 medium to large potatoes
110g (4oz) cheddar cheese, grated
50g (2oz) butter
60ml (4tbspn) soured cream
30ml (2tbspn) fresh chives, chopped
Salt and pepper

1 Scrub the potatoes and score around the middles with a sharp knife. Bake in an oven preheated to 200°C/400°F/Gas Mark 6 for about 1 hour 15 minutes or until tender. Cool for 10 minutes.

2 Cut the potatoes in half and, holding each half in a tea towel to protect your hands, carefully scoop the flesh into a bowl, leaving a thick-skinned shell.

3 Mash the potato until smooth, then mix in the butter and most of the cheese. Mix in the cream and chives and season to taste.

4 Pile the mixture back into the shells and arrange on a baking tray. Sprinkle with the remaining cheese. Return to the oven and bake for a further 15–20 minutes, until golden.

These potatoes make an excellent side dish but are also good with crispy bacon, diced ham, prawns or flaked tuna added for a light supper or lunch dish.

CAESAR'S SALAD

This classic salad is practically a meal in itself. Just serve with crusty bread for a light lunch or supper dish. You may notice Caesar's salad kits on your supermarket shelves, but this is such a simple recipe that making it from scratch is no problem.

SERVES: 4–6
PREPARATION TIME: 35 MINUTES + COOLING TIME

30ml (2tbspn) white wine vinegar
15ml (1tbspn) Worcestershire sauce
5ml (1tspn) salt
2.5ml (1/2tspn) ground black pepper
2.5ml (1/2tspn) mustard powder
5ml (1tspn) caster sugar
90ml (6tbspn) olive oil
2 cloves garlic, crushed
3 thick slices day-old white bread, crusts removed
45ml (3tbspn) vegetable oil
1 large, crisp lettuce
50g (2oz) parmesan cheese, finely grated
6 anchovy fillets, snipped into small pieces

DESSERTS

RECIPES

1

MOCHA FUDGE FLAN

A gooey chocolate and coffee flavoured filling in a biscuit crust.

2

PECAN PIE

A rich pastry case filled with pecan nuts in irresistible sticky maple syrup.

3

COFFEE CHIFFON PIE

A light coffee mousse in a crisp pastry shell.

4

CHOCOLATE FUDGE SUNDAE

Chocolate and vanilla ice cream layered with chopped walnuts and white chocolate chips and smothered in hot chocolate fudge sauce.

5

CREOLE PANCAKES

Banana slices in pancake parcels, surrounded by a buttery sauce, flavoured with orange, cinnamon and rum.

6

CRANBERRY AND ORANGE UPSIDE-DOWN PUDDING

Sharp cranberries baked with a rich sponge topping and turned out to give a delicious and colourful dessert.

7

OATY BLUEBERRY CRUMBLE

America's national fruit, served with a flapjack-style topping.

8

BLACKBERRY AND APPLE COBBLER

You can vary the fruit in this classic dish with its scone topping.

9

STUFFED PEACHES

Fresh peaches, stuffed and baked.

10

BLACK BOTTOM PIE

An attractive dessert, consisting of layers of chocolate and vanilla custard topped with whipped cream, in a pastry shell.

11

CHOCOLATE CHEESECAKE PIE

Like all the best American desserts, this is chocolatey, gooey and delicious.

12

BANANAS FOSTER

Bananas cooked in a rich buttery sauce and flambéed.

13

SHOO FLY PIE

A speciality of the Pennsylvanian Dutch settlers, this pie has a tasty spicy filling.

14

NEW YORK CHEESECAKE

Made famous by Lindy's delicatessen in New York, this cheesecake is flavoured with oranges and lemons and cooked in a rich pastry case.

15
KEY LIME PIE

A tangy and refreshing lime filling in a biscuit crust, topped with fluffy meringue.

16
PHILADELPHIA ICE CREAM

Rich and creamy, this recipe provides the basis of any number of flavour variations.

17
AMERICAN APPLE PIE

The most traditional of all American desserts, just like momma used to make!

18
STRAWBERRY SHORTCAKE

Buttery little shortcakes, split whilst warm and filled with cream and fresh strawberries.

19
BREAD PUDDING WITH WHISKY SAUCE

A traditional Creole dessert, good on its own but particularly scrumptious with the rich sauce.

20
BANANA CREAM PIE

Actually a cake rather than a pie, this is a light sponge filled with sliced bananas and a rich and creamy custard.

21
MISSISSIPPI MUD PIE

As the name suggests, this is a dense and gooey pudding – a rich chocolate filling in a crunchy biscuit crust.

MOCHA FUDGE FLAN

SERVES: 6
PREPARATION TIME: 20 MINUTES + CHILLING TIME

175g (6oz) digestive biscuits, crushed
75g (3oz) butter, melted
225g (8oz) plain chocolate, broken into pieces
5ml (1tspn) instant coffee powder
15ml (1tbspn) boiling water
50g (2oz) butter, softened
2 egg yolks
30ml (2tbspn) double cream
50g (2oz) walnuts, chopped

1 Mix together the crushed biscuits and melted butter until well blended. Press into the base and sides of an 18cm (7 inch) flan tin and chill until set.

2 Meanwhile, make the filling. Melt the chocolate in a bowl over hot water or in the microwave.

3 Dissolve the coffee in the boiling water and add to the melted chocolate. Stir in the butter until melted and then stir in the egg yolks and cream.

4 Mix in the chopped walnuts and turn the mixture into the biscuit case. Chill until set before serving.

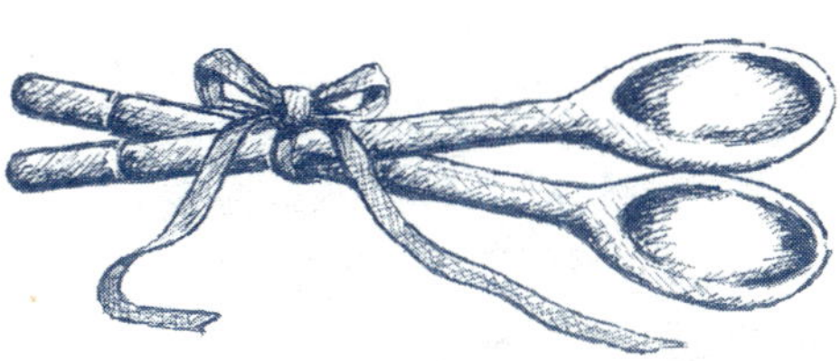

PECAN PIE

Pecans are very similar in appearance to walnuts, but have a slightly more subtle flavour and are less greasy. Try to use them in this recipe, although you can substitute walnuts if necessary.

SERVES: 6
PREPARATION TIME: 1 HOUR + STANDING TIME

PASTRY
225g (8oz) plain flour
Pinch of salt
175g (6oz) butter, diced
15ml (1tbspn) caster sugar
2 eggs, beaten

FILLING
3 eggs
15ml (1tbspn) milk
150ml (1/4pt) golden syrup
30ml (2tbspn) maple syrup
175g (6oz) soft brown sugar
50g (2oz) butter, melted
5ml (1tspn) vanilla extract
175g (6oz) nuts, half chopped and half left whole

1 Make the pastry by sifting the flour and salt into a bowl and rubbing in the butter until the mixture resembles fine breadcrumbs. Stir in the sugar. Add the beaten eggs and gradually, using first a knife and then your fingers, draw the mixture into a ball. Knead lightly for a minute or two, then wrap in cling film and chill for at least 45 minutes.

2 Roll out the chilled pastry and use to line a 22.5cm (9 inch) flan tin with a loose base. Rest the case for 5 minutes while making the filling.

3 Beat together the eggs and milk. Warm the syrups together with the sugar in a pan over a low heat. Slowly pour on to the egg mixture and beat in the butter and vanilla extract.

4 Scatter the chopped nuts over the base of the flan. Pour the syrup mixture over. Top with the whole nuts.

5 Bake in an oven preheated to 220°C/425°F/Gas Mark 7 for 10 minutes, then reduce the heat to 180°C/350°F/Gas Mark 4 and cook for a further 35–40 minutes, until the filling is set.

6 Serve warm or cold with cream or crème fraîche.

COFFEE CHIFFON PIE

Chiffon pies are popular in America and comprise a light mousse filling on a crisp pastry base. Fruit and chocolate flavours are popular, this coffee variety being slightly more unusual but equally delicious.

SERVES: 6
PREPARATION TIME: 1 HOUR 10 MINUTES

PASTRY
25g (1oz) caster sugar
75g (3oz) butter, softened
1 egg yolk
15ml (1tbspn) cold water
175g (6oz) plain flour
Pinch of salt

FILLING
10g (½oz) powdered gelatine
75ml (5tbspn) water
275ml (½pt) full cream milk
20ml (4tbspn) instant coffee powder
75g (3oz) caster sugar
2 eggs, separated
275ml (½pt) double cream

1 First make the pastry. In a large bowl, using your fingers, mix together the sugar, butter, egg yolk and water. Sift in the flour and salt and gradually work into the butter mixture to give a smooth dough. Wrap in cling film and chill for at least an hour.

2 Roll out the pastry to line a deep 20cm (8 inch) flan tin. Line the pastry case with greaseproof paper and weigh it down with dried beans or breadcrusts. Bake the case at 200°C/400°F/Gas Mark 6 for 20 minutes. Remove the weights and paper and bake for a further 5 minutes. Cool.

3 To make the filling, soak the gelatine in the water for 5 minutes, then dissolve over hot water or in the microwave.

4 Heat the milk and coffee until almost boiling. Beat together the sugar and egg yolks, add the hot milk and mix well. Return the total mix to the pan and cook gently over a low heat until it just thickens. Do not allow to boil. Add the gelatine to the mixture, strain into a large bowl and leave to cool.

5 Whisk the egg whites until stiff. When the custard is on the point of setting, fold in half the cream and the egg whites. Pour into the cooled pastry case and allow to set.

6 Whisk the remaining cream and use to pipe rosettes around the edge of the flan. Chill until ready to serve.

CHOCOLATE FUDGE SUNDAE

SERVES: 4
PREPARATION TIME: 15 MINUTES

275ml (½pt) vanilla ice cream
275ml (½pt) chocolate ice cream
50g (2oz) walnuts, chopped
Small bar white chocolate, roughly chopped
Small marshmallows (optional)

SAUCE
75ml (5tbspn) double cream
25g (1oz) cocoa powder
110g (4oz) soft brown sugar
175g (6oz) golden syrup
50g (2oz) butter
5ml (1tspn) vanilla extract

1 First make the sauce. Place all the ingredients except the vanilla extract in a small saucepan. Heat gently until the butter and sugar melt, then increase the heat and boil for 5 minutes.

2 Cool slightly, then add the vanilla extract.

3 Put a scoop of vanilla ice cream in each of 4 sundae dishes and add a sprinkling of chopped nuts. Top with a scoop of chocolate ice cream and some white chocolate pieces. Pour the sauce over the top and sprinkle with marshmallows, if using. Serve at once.

CREOLE PANCAKES

SERVES: 4
PREPARATION TIME: 30 MINUTES

PANCAKES
110g (4oz) plain flour
1 egg
275g (1/2pt) full cream milk
Oil for frying

FILLING
50g (2oz) butter
50g (2oz) dark soft brown sugar
45ml (3tbspn) dark rum
5ml (1tspn) ground cinnamon
Grated rind and juice 1 orange
3 large bananas, ripe but firm

1 First make the pancakes. Sieve the flour into a large bowl and make a well in the centre. Mix in the egg and gradually beat in the milk to make a smooth batter.

2 Heat a small amount of oil in a frying pan, pour in a little pancake batter and swirl the pan around until the batter thinly covers the base. Cook for about 1 minute, then flip the pancake over and cook the other side. Repeat to make about 8 pancakes. Layer the pancakes with greaseproof paper and keep warm.

3 To make the filling, place the butter, sugar, rum, cinnamon and orange rind and zest in a small pan and heat until the butter is melted and the sugar dissolved, stirring occasionally.

4 Peel the bananas and slice thinly. Stir into the sauce and heat gently for 5 minutes. Lift the banana slices out of the pan with a slotted spoon and divide between the pancakes. Fold the filled pancakes into parcels and arrange on a serving dish. Pour the sauce around and serve at once.

CRANBERRY AND ORANGE UPSIDE-DOWN PUDDING

SERVES: 6

PREPARATION TIME: 1 HOUR 15 MINUTES

25g (1oz) butter, melted
275g (10oz) cranberries
75g (3oz) soft brown sugar
30ml (2tbspn) orange juice
225g (8oz) self-raising flour
5ml (1tspn) baking powder
1 egg
Grated rind and juice of 1 large orange
45ml (3tbspn) milk
110g (4oz) butter, softened
110g (4oz) caster sugar

1 Grease a 22.5cm (9 inch) round cake tin with a solid base. Pour in the melted butter. Mix together the cranberries, brown sugar and orange juice and spread this mixture over the butter in the base of the tin.

2 Sift the flour and baking powder into a large bowl. Add the remaining ingredients and beat until the mixture is smooth and glossy. Spoon over the cranberry mixture and level the top.

3 Bake at 180°C/350°F/Gas Mark 6 for about an hour, until well risen and firm to the touch.

4 Cool in the tin for a few minutes, then turn out carefully on to a serving plate. Serve whilst still warm, with cream or ice cream.

OATY BLUEBERRY CRUMBLE

Blueberries are practically the national fruit of America. It is now possible to buy blueberries in larger supermarkets, both fresh and frozen, but blackberries, raspberries or blackcurrants work well too.

SERVES: 6
PREPARATION TIME: 55 MINUTES

FILLING
900g (2lb) blueberries
50g (2oz) caster sugar
15ml (1tbspn) cornflour
15ml (1tbspn) lemon juice

TOPPING
110g (4oz) butter
110g (4oz) plain flour
110g (4oz) soft brown sugar
75g (3oz) rolled oats
Pinch of ground cinnamon
50g (2oz) walnuts, chopped

1 Place the blueberries in a pan and heat gently until the juices start to flow. Stir in the sugar. Mix together the cornflour and lemon juice and mix into the fruit. Bring to the boil, stirring, remove from the heat and transfer the mixture to a pie dish.

2 For the crumble, sift the flour into a bowl and rub in the butter until the mixture resembles coarse breadcrumbs. Stir in the sugar, oats, cinnamon and nuts and spoon the mixture over the fruit.

3 Bake at 190°C/375°F/Gas Mark 5 for about 35 minutes, until golden brown. Serve warm with cream, custard or ice cream.

BLACKBERRY AND APPLE COBBLER

SERVES: 4
PREPARATION TIME: 45 MINUTES

450g (1lb) cooking apples
450g (1lb) blackberries
Pinch of ground cinnamon
75g (3oz) granulated sugar
225g (8oz) self-raising flour
50g (2oz) butter
25g (1oz) caster sugar
Milk to mix
Demerara sugar

1 Peel and core the apples and cut into thin slices. Place them in a saucepan with the blackberries and cinnamon. Heat gently to release the juices and simmer until the fruit is tender. Stir in the granulated sugar and cool.

2 Sift the flour into a bowl, stir in the sugar and rub in the butter until the mixture resembles breadcrumbs. Add enough milk to make a soft dough.

3 Roll out the dough on a lightly floured work surface to about 1cm (1/2 inch) thick. Cut out rounds using a 5cm (2 inch) cutter. Roll the trimmings out again to make more rounds.

4 Transfer the fruit to a pie dish and top with the scone rounds, overlapping them and leaving the centre uncovered. Brush the rounds with milk and sprinkle with demerara sugar.

5 Bake at 220°C/425°F/Gas Mark 7 for 15 minutes, until the topping is golden brown. Serve hot with cream or ice cream.

STUFFED PEACHES

This is a delicious but quick and simple dessert that makes the most of the succulent fresh peaches readily available in the southern states of America.

SERVES: 4
PREPARATION TIME: 30 MINUTES

4 large ripe peaches
90ml (6tbspn) cake or biscuit crumbs
30ml (2tbspn) brandy
90ml (6tbspn) apricot jam
50g (2oz) flaked almonds

1 First skin the peaches. Cut them in half and remove the stones, then place in a bowl and cover with boiling water. Leave for two minutes, then drain off the boiling water and cover with cold water. The skins should then peel away quite easily – you will find the cut edges give a good starting point.

2 Mix together the cake or biscuit crumbs, the brandy and half the apricot jam. Divide this mixture between 4 of the peach halves and sandwich with the remaining 4 halves.

3 Stand the peaches in a lightly greased, shallow oven-proof dish. Brush over the remaining jam and sprinkle with the almonds.

4 Bake at 190°C/375°F/Gas Mark 5 for 15 minutes. Serve hot with cream or ice cream.

BLACK BOTTOM PIE

This dessert looks particularly attractive when it is cut, with layers of dark and light filling and whipped cream topping.

SERVES: 8
PREPARATION TIME: 1 HOUR + CHILLING TIME

PASTRY
175g (6oz) plain flour
25g (1oz) icing sugar
75g (3oz) butter
1 egg yolk
Cold water

FILLING
10g (½oz) powdered gelatine
30ml (2tbspn) cold water
4 eggs, separated
75ml (3tbspn) plain flour
25g (1oz) soft brown sugar
425ml (¾pt) full cream milk
150g (5oz) plain chocolate
30ml (2tbspn) cocoa powder
30ml (2tbspn) brandy
75g (3oz) caster sugar
150ml (¼pt) double cream
Grated plain chocolate for decoration

1 First make the pastry case. Sift the flour and icing sugar into a bowl. Rub in the butter until the mixture resembles fine breadcrumbs. Add the egg yolk and enough water to make a firm dough.

2 Roll out the pastry on a floured work surface and use to line a 22.5cm (9 inch) round, loose-based flan tin. Prick the base lightly with a fork. Line with greaseproof paper and weigh down with dry beans or bread crusts. Bake at 200°C/400°F/Gas Mark 6 for 20 minutes. Remove the weights and paper and bake for a further 5–10 minutes, until golden brown. Cool.

3 Beat together the egg yolks, brown sugar and plain flour until smooth. Heat the milk in a heavy based saucepan, pour over the egg yolks and mix well. Return to the saucepan, bring to the boil, stirring, and simmer for 5 minutes.

4 Measure 275ml (1/2pt) of this custard into a bowl. Add the chocolate and stir until melted. Add the cocoa and half the brandy. Cool, then pour into the flan case. Chill.

5 Place the gelatine in a small bowl with the water and dissolve over hot water or in the microwave.

6 Add the gelatine to the remaining custard with the rest of the brandy. Whisk the egg whites until stiff and whisk in the sugar. Fold this mixture into the custard and carefully pour it over the chocolate layer in the flan case. Refrigerate for 2 hours.

7 Whip the cream until thick and spread it over the top of the flan. Decorate with grated chocolate.

CHOCOLATE CHEESECAKE PIE

This is a dessert that can be made extremely quickly and is bound to be a hit with all chocolate lovers.

SERVES: 6
PREPARATION TIME: 50 MINUTES

110g (4oz) digestive biscuits
40g (1½ oz) butter, melted
350g (12oz) full fat soft cheese
225g (8oz) caster sugar
40g (1½ oz) cocoa powder
Pinch of ground cinnamon
3 eggs
90ml (6tbspn) double cream

1 Crush the biscuits. (Putting them in a plastic bag and running a rolling pin over it is an effective method.) Transfer the crumbs to a bowl and add the melted butter, mixing well to evenly cover the crumbs. Press the mixture into the base of a 20cm (8 inch) loose-based flan tin.

2 To make the filling, place the cheese in a bowl and beat until smooth and softened. Add the sugar and sift in the cocoa powder and cinnamon. Mix well. Beat in the eggs with the cream until the mixture is just smooth. Pour into the flan tin on top of the crumbs.

3 Bake at 180°C/350°F/Gas Mark 4 for 30 minutes, until the filling is puffed up. Cool to room temperature before serving, when the filling will sink down.

BANANAS FOSTER

This dish, originally created in a restaurant in New Orleans, makes a spectacular yet simple dessert. Don't be put off by the thought of flambéeing. You probably do it every year with your Christmas pudding anyway. This recipe looks just as impressive if you bring it to the table while it is still alight. Make sure you have all the ingredients to hand before you start cooking, as it all happens very quickly.

SERVES: 4
PREPARATION TIME: 15 MINUTES

4 large bananas, ripe but not squashy
110g (4oz) butter, cut into small cubes
110g (4oz) soft brown sugar
2.5ml (1/2 tspn) ground cinnamon
Vanilla ice cream to serve
90ml (6tbspn) rum, preferably white

1 Peel the bananas and half them lengthwise.

2 Heat a large frying pan over a medium to high heat. Add the butter and sugar and melt together to make a smooth sauce. Stir in the cinnamon.

3 Add the bananas and cook gently in the syrup for about 4 minutes, pouring the syrup over them as they cook.

4 Place scoops of ice cream in 4 dishes.

5 Warm the rum, either in a small pan or in the microwave. Add to the pan and quickly ignite.

6 Dish up 2 banana halves and plenty of syrup with the ice cream.

SHOO FLY PIE

This pie was introduced by the Dutch settlers to Pennsylvania. With all those sticky ingredients, there is no need to wonder where the name came from.

SERVES: 6
PREPARATION TIME: 50 MINUTES

PASTRY
175g (6oz) plain flour
25g (1oz) icing sugar
75g (3oz) butter
1 egg yolk
Cold water to mix

BASE AND TOPPING
90g (3½ oz) plain flour
90g (3½ oz) soft dark brown sugar
2.5ml (½ tspn) ground ginger
2.5ml (½ tspn) ground cinnamon
2.5ml (½ tspn) grated nutmeg
50g (2oz) butter

FILLING
2 eggs
125ml (4 fl oz) black treacle – or for a milder flavour replace any proportion of this with golden syrup
125ml (4 fl oz) boiling water
2.5ml (½ tspn) bicarbonate of soda
Brown sugar

1 First make the pastry. Sift the flour and icing sugar into a bowl and rub in the butter until the mixture resembles fine breadcrumbs. Add the egg yolk and enough cold water to make a firm dough. Knead lightly and roll out the pastry on a lightly floured work surface. Use to line a 22.5cm (9 inch) round flan tin.

2 For the topping, mix together the flour, sugar and spices in a bowl. Cut the butter into small pieces and rub into the flour until the mixture looks like coarse crumbs. Spoon about a third of this mixture into the pastry case.

3 For the filling, whisk the eggs with the treacle. Stir the bicarbonate of soda into the boiling water and immediately add to the egg mix (it will be foaming) and mix well.

4 Quickly pour the treacle mix into the pastry case and top with the remaining crumbs as evenly as possible. Sprinkle with brown sugar.

5 Bake in an oven preheated to 190°C/375°F/Gas Mark 5 for 35 minutes. Serve warm with cream or ice cream.

NEW YORK CHEESECAKE

SERVES: 10
PREPARATION TIME: 2 HOURS 30 MINUTES + COOLING TIME

PASTRY
125g (4½oz) plain flour
125g (4½oz) butter, diced
40g (1½oz) caster sugar
15ml (1tbspn) grated lemon zest
1 egg yolk

FILLING
900g (2lb) curd cheese
350g (12oz) caster sugar
40g (1½oz) plain flour
45ml (3tbspn) grated orange zest
30ml (2tbspn) grated lemon zest
3 egg yolks
5 eggs
150ml (¼pt) double cream
Icing sugar to dust

1 First make the pastry. Sift the flour into a bowl, rub in the butter and stir in the sugar and zest. Add the egg yolk and work together to form a dough. Knead lightly, wrap in cling film and chill for 30 minutes.

2 Roll out half the pastry and use it to line the base of a 25cm (10 inch) spring-form tin. Prick lightly with a fork and bake at 220°C/425°F/Gas Mark 7 for 10–15 minutes, until golden brown. Cool. Roll the remaining pastry into a strip the depth and circumference of the tin. Arrange along the inside, pressing gently on to the pastry base.

3 Beat together the cheese, sugar and flour. Beat in the orange and lemon zests and the egg yolks. Gradually beat in the eggs, one at a time and then the cream.

4 Pour the mixture into the pastry case and bake for 15 minutes. Reduce the heat to 110°C/225°F/Gas Mark ¼ and cook for a further 1¼–1½ hours until set. Test by inserting a thin skewer into the centre of the mix – it should come out clean. Cool in the tin, on a wire rack, and chill, preferably overnight.

5 Remove carefully from the tin and dust with icing sugar.

KEY LIME PIE

SERVES: 6
PREPARATION TIME: 40 MINUTES + COOLING TIME

BASE AND FILLING
175g (6oz) digestive biscuits, crushed
75g (3oz) butter, melted
220g (7oz) caster sugar
25g (1oz) butter
25g (1oz) cornflour
Juice and finely grated zest of 4 limes
3 egg yolks

MERINGUE
150g (5oz) caster sugar
3 egg whites

1 Mix the biscuits and melted butter together and press into the base and up the sides of a deep 20cm (8 inch) flan dish.

2 To make the filling, place the sugar and butter in a saucepan with 275ml (1/2pt) of water. Heat gently until the sugar has dissolved and the butter has melted. Blend the cornflour with the lime juice and zest and add to the saucepan, stirring vigorously. Bring to the boil, stirring all the time until the mixture has thickened. Stir in the egg yolks, mixing well, and leave to cool. Pour into the biscuit base.

3 To make the meringue, whisk the egg whites until stiff. Gradually whisk in the sugar 15ml (1tbspn) at a time until the mixture is thick.

4 Pile the meringue on to the lime filling, spreading it out to the edges to seal the filling in. Use a palette knife to lift the meringue into peaks.

5 Bake at 200°C/400°F/Gas Mark 6 for 15–20 minutes, until the meringue is golden brown. Cool before serving.

PHILADELPHIA ICE CREAM

This recipe can be made without special equipment, but if you have an ice cream maker, just place the mixture in it as normal at stage 2.

SERVES: 4–6
PREPARATION TIME: 10 MINUTES + FREEZING TIME

425ml (3/4pt) single cream
200g (7oz) caster sugar
425ml (3/4pt) double cream
10ml (2tspn) vanilla extract

1 Heat the single cream and sugar together in a pan over a low heat until the sugar has dissolved. Cool.

2 Mix in the double cream and the vanilla extract and turn the mixture into a shallow plastic tray. Place in the deep freeze at the coldest setting.

3 Leave the ice cream for about an hour, until the edges start to freeze, then whisk briskly with a fork. Freeze again for an hour and whisk again. Repeat this process until the whole mixture is a thick, frozen "slush". Now freeze for 3–4 hours until solid. Cover.

4 Transfer to the main body of the refrigerator for about half an hour before serving.

AMERICAN APPLE PIE

"As American as apple pie!" This has to be one of the best known American dishes, although there are probably hundreds of variations. American pastry has a higher fat content than the shortcrust pastry we usually make.

SERVES: 6
PREPARATION TIME: 1 HOUR 15 MINUTES

225g (8oz) self-raising flour
2.5ml (1/2 tspn) salt
110g (4oz) butter
40g (1 1/2 oz) lard or white vegetable fat
60–75ml (4–5tbspn) iced water
1 egg, beaten
6–7 eating apples, peeled, cored and sliced
75g (3oz) caster sugar
5ml (1tspn) ground cinnamon
Pinch of ground nutmeg
Zest of 1 lemon

1 Sift the flour and salt into a bowl. Cut the butter and lard into small pieces and rub into the flour until the mixture resembles fine breadcrumbs.

2 Add the iced water and mix until a dough begins to form. You may need to use a little more water if it looks too dry. Wrap in cling film and chill for at least 20 minutes.

3 Roll out half the pastry and use it to line a 20–22.5cm (8–9 inch) round pie plate. Brush the pastry with beaten egg.

4 Combine apple slices, sugar, spices and lemon zest and pile into the pie dish. Brush the edge with egg. Roll out the remaining pastry and cover the apples. Seal the edges and trim off any excess pastry. Brush the top with beaten egg and cut a vent in the centre.

5 Bake at 220°C/425°F/Gas Mark 7 for 10 minutes. Reduce the heat to 180°C/350°F/Gas Mark 4 and bake for a further 30–35 minutes, until the pastry is golden brown and the fruit is soft (check with a sharp knife through the vent hole). Serve warm. Vanilla ice cream is a delicious accompaniment.

STRAWBERRY SHORTCAKES

SERVES: 6
PREPARATION TIME: 40 MINUTES

225g (8oz) plain flour
15ml (1tbspn) caster sugar
Pinch of salt
15ml (1tbspn) baking powder
110g (4oz) butter, cut into small pieces
150ml (1/4pt) full cream milk
1 egg, beaten
575ml (1pt) double cream
450–700g (1–1 1/2lb) strawberries, sliced, except for 6 left whole for garnishing
Icing sugar and butter to serve.

1 Sift the flour, sugar, salt and baking powder into a bowl. Rub the butter into the flour until the mixture resembles fine breadcrumbs.

2 Add the milk and most of the egg. Mix to a soft dough.

3 Roll out the dough on a floured surface to 1cm (1/2 inch) thick. Cut into 6 rounds, 8cm (3 inches) in diameter, rolling the trimmings again as necessary. Place the rounds on a lightly greased baking tray and brush with the remaining beaten egg.

4 Bake in an oven preheated to 220°C/425°F/Gas Mark 7 for 12–15 minutes, until golden brown.

5 To serve, split the warm shortcakes in half and spread thinly with butter. Beat the cream until thick. Place a large spoonful of whipped cream on each base, cover with a mound of sliced strawberries and top with more cream. Add the "lid" and top with a blob of cream and a strawberry. Dust with icing sugar and serve.

BREAD PUDDING WITH WHISKY SAUCE

SERVES: 4–6
PREPARATION TIME: 1 HOUR 15 MINUTES

PUDDING
1 small French stick
50g (2oz) butter
50g (2oz) raisins or sultanas
4 eggs
110g (4oz) caster sugar
5ml (1tspn) vanilla extract
275ml (½pt) full cream milk
275ml (½pt) double cream
15ml (1tbspn) whisky

SAUCE
110g (4oz) butter
1 egg
175g (6oz) caster sugar
90ml (6tbspn) whisky

1 Slice the bread into thin slices and butter on one side. Arrange in a lightly buttered oven-proof dish, sprinkling with raisins between layers, but not on the top.

2 Whisk the eggs and sugar together with the vanilla extract. Place the milk and cream in a pan and heat until almost boiling. Pour over the eggs, stirring all the while. Stir in the whisky. Pour the custard over the bread and leave to stand for 30 minutes.

3 Place the dish in a roasting pan of water so that the water comes halfway up the sides of the dish. Bake at 180°C/350°F/Gas Mark 4 for 25–30 minutes, until just firm to the touch.

4 Meanwhile, make the sauce. Place a bowl over a pan of simmering water and add the butter. Heat until melted, then whisk in the egg and sugar and continue whisking until the mixture thickens. Cool slightly, then stir in the whisky. Serve with the hot pudding.

BANANA CREAM PIE

This "pie" is really a cake. It is a light sponge, filled with bananas and a rich custard and topped with chocolate.

SERVES: 8
PREPARATION TIME: 1 HOUR 30 MINUTES + CHILLING TIME

CAKE
50g (2oz) butter, melted
4 eggs
110g (4oz) caster sugar
2.5ml (1/2 tspn) vanilla extract
110g (4oz) plain flour, sifted

FILLING
275ml (1/2 pt) full cream milk
2.5ml (1/2 tspn) vanilla extract
4 egg yolks
60g (2 1/2 oz) caster sugar
30ml (2tbspn) plain flour
1 large banana, ripe but firm

TOPPING
150ml ($^1/_4$pt) double cream
110g (4oz) plain chocolate

1 To make the cake, grease a 22.5cm (9 inch) round cake tin and line the base with baking parchment. Place the eggs in a large bowl and set it over a pan of simmering water. Add the sugar and beat, preferably with an electric whisk, until the mixture doubles in volume and is so thick that it leaves a trail when you lift the whisk out. Fold in the flour with a large metal spoon. Finally, fold in the melted butter and turn the mixture into the prepared tin. Bake at 180°C/350°F/Gas Mark 4 for 35 minutes, until just firm to the touch. Carefully turn out on to a wire rack to cool.

2 To make the filling, heat the milk in a heavy based saucepan. Beat the egg yolks and sugar together in a bowl until they are light and fluffy and stir in the flour. Whisk the hot milk into the egg mixture, add the vanilla essence and return the mixture to the pan. Heat gently until the cream thickens. Simmer for 2–3 minutes, then turn into a bowl to cool. Cover with cling film to prevent a skin forming.

3 When the cake is cool, slice it into two even layers. Place the bottom half on a plate. Cover with the pastry cream and top with the sliced banana. Place the other half of the cake on top.

4 To make the glaze, melt the chocolate, either in a bowl over hot water or in the microwave. Whisk the melted chocolate quickly into the cream and spread over the top of the cake. Chill the cake before serving.

MISSISSIPPI MUD PIE

SERVES: 8–10 (DEPENDING HOW SWEET-TOOTHED YOUR GUESTS ARE)
PREPARATION TIME: 1 HOUR 30 MINUTES

BASE
110g (4oz) ginger biscuits
110g (4oz) digestive biscuits
75g (3oz) butter, melted
25g (1oz) soft brown sugar

FILLING
225g (8oz) butter
175g (6oz) plain chocolate
90ml (6tbspn) golden syrup
4 eggs, beaten
50g (2oz) walnuts, chopped

1 Crush the biscuits. It is best to do the two kinds separately, as digestives crush easily, but ginger biscuits can put up a bit of a fight. Place the crumbs in a bowl and mix in the melted butter and sugar. Press this mixture into the base of a 22.5cm (9 inch) diameter loose-based cake tin and chill.

2 To make the filling, put the butter, chocolate and syrup into a heavy based saucepan and heat very gently until all the ingredients are just melted and combined. Cool, then mix in the beaten eggs and chopped walnuts. Pour on to the biscuit base.

3 Bake at 180°C/350°F/Gas Mark 4 for about 60–75 minutes, until the filling is just firm but still slightly soft – this makes the finished dessert suitably gooey. Serve warm or cold with ice cream or cream.

Baking

RECIPES

1

FROSTED WALNUT LAYER CAKE

Moist walnut sponge, sandwiched with buttercream and coated in traditional American frosting.

2

DOUGHNUTS

A basic recipe with a number of wicked variations.

3

APPLESAUCE CAKE

A moist and spicy cake that is delicious on its own or can be sliced and buttered as a tea loaf.

4

POUND CAKE

A traditional recipe that gives a rich, plain cake.

5

LACE COOKIES

Elegant and crispy, it is their light, delicate texture that gives these biscuits their name. Try them with ice cream or fruity desserts.

6

SNICKERDOODLES

Buttery plain biscuits rolled in cinnamon sugar to give a crisp finish.

7
COFFEE CAKE

Not coffee flavoured, but designed to be eaten with a cup of coffee, this cake has a spicy, nutty filling and topping.

8
DANISH PASTRIES

Once you have sampled homemade Danish pastries, the bought variety will never taste the same again.

9
QUICK CHOCOLATE FUDGE

A foolproof and painless chocolate fudge recipe with a number of delicious variations.

10
ANGEL CAKE

The lightest of all cakes, baked in a ring. Add fruit and whipped cream to make a luscious dessert.

11
CHOCOLATE LAYER CAKE

A rich chocolate layer cake. Choose either chocolate fudge icing or traditional American frosting to fill and top it.

12
BLUEBERRY CINNAMON CAKE

A tasty cake, juicy with blueberries and with a nutty crumble topping.

13
CHOCOLATE PEANUT BROWNIES

Like all good brownies, these should be slightly undercooked, so that they are rich and gooey.

14
CORNBREAD

Served in America with all sorts of meals, from chillies to chicken, it is also the basis of the classic Thanksgiving cornbread stuffing.

15
MUFFINS
Here are the basic recipes for sweet and savoury muffins and some ideas for flavourings you could use.

16
CINNAMON PECAN ROLLS
Little yeast buns rolled around a spicy, nutty filling. Delicious warm from the oven for brunch.

17
CHOCOLATE CHIP COOKIES
Famous little biscuits that need no introduction. A favourite with adults and children alike.

18
CRANBERRY LOAF
Sharp and juicy cranberries mixed into a moist, orange-flavoured loaf.

19
MARSHMALLOW CRISPIES
Americans include marshmallows in many recipes, both sweet and savoury, of which these little cakes, popular with children, are a great example.

20
CARROT CAKE
A nutty cake, tangy with orange and lemon juice and moist with carrots, with an unusual cream cheese and honey frosting.

21
SPICY SOURED CREAM COOKIES
Chewy and spicy little biscuits, an ideal Christmas treat.

FROSTED WALNUT LAYER CAKE

SERVES: 8
PREPARATION TIME: 1 HOUR

CAKE
175g (6oz) butter, softened
175g (6oz) soft brown sugar
3 eggs, beaten
175g (6oz) self-raising flour
110g (4oz) walnuts, chopped

FILLING
110g (4oz) butter, softened
225g (8oz) icing sugar
50g (2oz) walnuts, finely chopped

FROSTING
225g (8oz) granulated sugar
60ml (4tbspn) water
1 egg white
Walnut halves

1 First make the cake. Cream together the butter and soft brown sugar until light and fluffy. Gradually beat in the eggs, then fold in the flour and walnuts. Divide the mixture between 3 greased and lined 18cm (7 inch) round sponge tins.

2 Bake at 190°C/375°F/Gas Mark 5 for 20–25 minutes, until well risen and just firm to the touch. Carefully turn out of the tins and cool on wire racks.

3 Meanwhile, make the filling. Beat together the butter and icing

sugar until light and fluffy. Stir in the walnuts. When cool, sandwich together the cakes with the buttercream.

4 To make the frosting, heat together the sugar and water until the sugar has dissolved. Bring to the boil and boil for about 10 minutes, until the mixture becomes syrupy but not coloured.

5 Whisk the egg white until stiff, then gradually pour the syrup on to the egg white, whisking all the time. Continue whisking until the mixture thickens, then very quickly spread over the top and sides of the cake and decorate with walnut halves.

DOUGHNUTS

Doughnuts are the ultimate American snack and the choice of flavours is bewildering. The following recipe is a starting point. The rest is up to your own imagination!

MAKES: ABOUT 16 DOUGHNUTS
PREPARATION TIME: 2½ HOURS, INCLUDING PROVING TIME

25g (1oz) fresh yeast
50g (2oz) caster sugar
275ml (½pt) full cream milk, warmed
450g (1lb) strong plain flour
5ml (1tspn) salt
50g (2oz) butter
1 egg, beaten
Oil for deep frying

1 In a bowl, cream together the yeast and sugar and then mix in the warm milk and 110g (4oz) of the flour. Leave to stand in a warm place for 20 minutes, until beginning to froth.

2 Sift the rest of the flour into a large bowl with the salt and rub in the butter. Make a well in the centre and add the egg and the yeast mixture.

3 Using first a wooden spoon and then your hands, begin to work the flour into the liquid to make a rough dough. When it is all mixed in, turn the dough on to a floured work surface and knead until it becomes smooth and elastic.

4 Return the dough to a lightly floured bowl, cover with a clean tea towel and leave in a warm place for about an hour, until the mixture has doubled in size.

5 Turn the dough out on to a floured work surface and knead again. The dough is now ready to be shaped. You can roll it into fat sausages, flatten them into oblongs, or knead the mixture into balls. To make rings, roll out the dough to about 2cm (3/4 inch) thick. First cut out rounds using a 7.5cm (3 inch) cutter and then cut out the middles using a 4cm (1 1/2 inch) cutter. Leave your chosen shapes in a warm place for 20 minutes.

6 Meanwhile, heat the oil in a deep-fat fryer or a large, heavy based saucepan to 108°C/350°F. Fry about 3 doughnuts at a time, turning them over halfway through, to give a well risen, golden brown doughnut. Lift out and drain on kitchen paper.

7 To eat the doughnuts warm, toss them in cinnamon sugar. Mix 60ml (4tbspn) caster sugar with 5ml (1tspn) ground cinnamon and place in a paper bag. Add the warm doughnuts, one at a time, and shake until well coated. Do not be tempted to use a plastic bag – an unpleasant mess results when the hot doughnut melts through the bag!

8 American doughnuts are usually filled and topped. You will find some suggestions below. To fill a doughnut, push the handle of a wooden spoon into the cooked doughnut to make a channel and then fill, using a piping bag with a suitably sized nozzle.

Lemon Doughnuts

Fill the doughnuts with lemon curd (homemade is best) and top with lemon icing. Mix icing sugar with lemon juice to make a thick paste. Add a few drops of yellow food colouring and spread over the top of the doughnuts.

Apple Doughnuts

Peel and core a cooking apple and cut into small cubes. Place in a saucepan with a small amount of water and cook until tender. Add sugar to taste, cool and use to fill doughnuts. Brush the tops of the doughnuts with apricot jam and sprinkle with flaked almonds.

Mocha Doughnuts

Melt 110g (4oz) plain chocolate over hot water or in the microwave. Cool, then mix with 150ml ($^1/_4$pt) of double cream. Beat until thick and use to fill doughnuts. Top with coffee icing. Dissolve 5ml (1tspn) of instant coffee powder in 15ml (1tbspn) of hot water. Add enough icing sugar to make a stiff paste and spread over the top of the doughnuts. Sprinkle with chocolate vermicelli.

Jam Doughnuts

Simply fill the doughnuts with the jam of your choice. Top with vanilla icing if you wish. Mix icing sugar with water to make a stiff paste. Add a few drops of vanilla extract and spread over the top of the doughnuts. Sprinkle with hundreds and thousands.

APPLESAUCE CAKE

SERVES: 10
PREPARATION TIME: 1 HOUR 45 MINUTES

2 cooking apples, peeled and cored
110g (4oz) butter
175g (6oz) soft brown sugar
1 egg, beaten
200g (7oz) self-raising flour
Pinch of salt
5ml (1tspn) ground cinnamon
2.5ml (1/2 tspn) ground cloves
175g (6oz) raisins
75g (3oz) walnuts, chopped

1 Cut the apples into slices and place in a pan with a dash of water. Heat gently until soft. Add more water if necessary but try to keep the mixture as dry as possible. Cool. Drain any moisture from the apples and mash to a pulp.

2 Meanwhile, cream together the butter and sugar in a bowl until light and fluffy, and beat in the egg.

3 Sift together the flour, salt and spices and fold into the butter mixture. Stir in the raisins, walnuts and apple pulp.

4 Turn the mixture into a greased and lined 900g (2lb) loaf tin and bake at 180°C/350°F/Gas Mark 4 for about 1 1/2 hours, until risen and firm to the touch. Cool in the tin for a few minutes, then carefully turn out and finish cooling on a wire rack.

5 Serve plain or sliced and buttered.

POUND CAKE

These rich plain cakes were probably originally so named because the recipe called for a pound of each of the main ingredients. This would make an enormous cake by today's standards, so this recipe has been adjusted to more manageable quantities.

SERVES: 12
PREPARATION TIME: 1 HOUR 45 MINUTES + COOLING TIME

225g (8oz) butter
450g (1lb) caster sugar
4 eggs, beaten
350g (12oz) self-raising flour
Pinch of salt
215ml (7.5fl oz) full cream milk
5ml (1tspn) vanilla extract

1 Cream the butter and sugar until light and fluffy. Gradually beat in the eggs.

2 Sift the flour and salt together and gradually add to the egg mixture, alternating with the milk, until all the flour and milk is incorporated into the mix. Stir in the vanilla extract.

3 Turn the mixture into a greased and lined 22.5cm (9 inch) round cake tin and bake in an oven preheated to 180°C/350°F/Gas Mark 4 for about $1^1/2$ hours, until risen and firm to the touch.

4 Allow to cool in the tin for 10 minutes, then turn on to a wire rack to finish cooling.

COFFEE CAKE

American coffee cakes are not coffee flavoured. They are intended to be eaten with a cup of coffee. They are ideal for a mid-morning snack or with a late-night hot drink.

SERVES: 12
PREPARATION TIME: 1 HOUR 30 MINUTES

FILLING AND TOPPING
175g (6oz) soft brown sugar
10ml (2tspn) ground cinnamon
150g (5oz) walnuts, chopped
50g (2oz) butter, melted

CAKE
110g (4oz) butter
110g (4oz) soft brown sugar
3 eggs, beaten
225g (8oz) self-raising flour
5ml (1tspn) bicarbonate of soda
275ml (1/2pt) soured cream

1 First make the topping and filling – the same mixture is used for both. Blend together the sugar, cinnamon and walnuts and stir in the melted butter. Leave to cool, stirring occasionally to break up the mixture.

2 For the cake, cream together the butter and sugar until light and fluffy. Gradually beat in the eggs.

3 Sift together the flour and bicarbonate of soda and alternately add to the butter mixture with the soured cream.

4 Place half this mixture in a greased and lined 22.5cm (9 inch) square cake tin and level. Sprinkle with half the topping mixture. Cover with the remaining cake mixture and sprinkle with the remaining topping.

5 Bake at 180°C/350°F/Gas Mark 4 for about an hour, until well risen and firm. Cool in the tin for 5 minutes, then carefully turn out and cool on a rack. This is delicious eaten warm.

DANISH PASTRIES

Coffee and a Danish is a standard mid-morning snack in America – deadly to the dieter but delicious! Danish pastries look complicated to make but taken a stage at a time are really quite easy. The process is a combination of making bread and flaky pastry and the results are so good that you are sure to think the time spent kneading and rolling was well spent.

The recipe below suggests four different fillings for the same batch of dough. Of course, you can double the quantities of one and leave out another, or use only one filling, increasing the quantities as necessary.

MAKES: ABOUT 12 PASTRIES
PREPARATION TIME: 1 HOUR 30 MINUTES

DOUGH
25g (1oz) fresh yeast
50g (2oz) caster sugar
150ml (1/4pt) full cream milk, warmed
450g (1lb) strong plain flour
275g (10oz) butter
2 eggs, beaten

FILLINGS AND TOPPINGS
50g (2oz) butter
50g (2oz) soft brown sugar
10ml (2tspn) ground cinnamon
50g (2oz) currants
110g (4oz) ground almonds
110g (4oz) caster sugar
1 egg, beaten
1 small can apricot halves, drained
1 cooking apple
Caster sugar
Apricot jam, sieved
Flaked almonds
Glacé cherries

1 First make the dough. Cream together the yeast and sugar, then blend in the warm milk and 110g (4oz) of the flour. Leave in a warm place for 20 minutes, until starting to froth.

2 Sift the remaining flour into a bowl. Add 50g (2oz) of the butter and rub in until the mixture resembles breadcrumbs. Make a well in the centre and add the beaten eggs and the yeast mixture. Using first a wooden spoon and then your hands, work the mixture together to form a rough dough, then turn out on to a floured work surface and knead until smooth and elastic.

3 Shape the remaining butter into a block. Roll out the dough to an oblong, place the butter in the centre and flip over the ends of the dough to enclose the butter. Now turn the dough through 90° and roll out again to an oblong. Mark the dough into three even sections, then fold one end over the middle and cover with the other end (see illustration below). Roll out again to an oblong and repeat this process three more times. It is this process that gives the cooked dough its flaky texture, so don't skimp on the rolling and folding. Wrap the dough in cling film and chill for at least 30 minutes, while making the fillings.

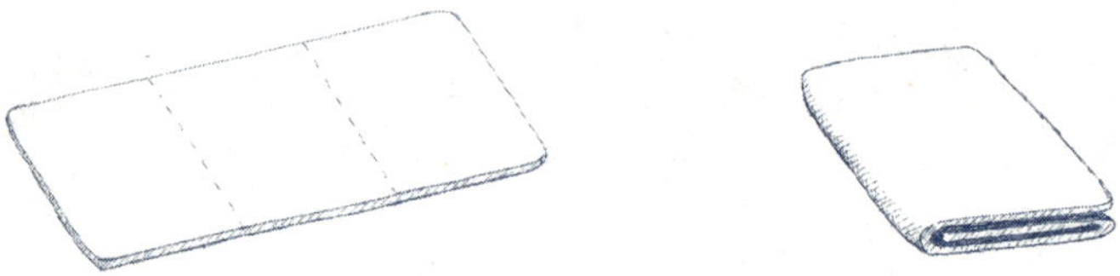

4 To make the fruit filling, cream together the butter and soft brown sugar with the cinnamon. Mix in the currants.

5 To make the almond and apricot filling, mix the ground almonds and caster sugar with enough beaten egg to make a smooth paste.

6 To make the apple filling, peel and core the apple and chop into small pieces. Place in a pan with a very little water and cook until tender. Add sugar to taste and cool.

7 Roll out the chilled dough to about 5mm ($^1/_4$ inch) thick. Cut an oblong 15cm x 30cm (6 inches x 12 inches). Spread with the currant mixture and roll up from the short end, as you would a swiss roll (see the illustration below). Cut into 1cm ($^1/_2$ inch) slices to make whirls. Place on a greased baking tray.

8 From the rolled-out dough, cut 10cm (4 inch) squares. Cut from each corner towards the centre about 3cm ($1^1/_4$ inches). Place a spoonful of almond paste in the centre and top with an apricot half. Lift every alternate point towards the centre to make a windmill (see below). Place on a greased baking tray.

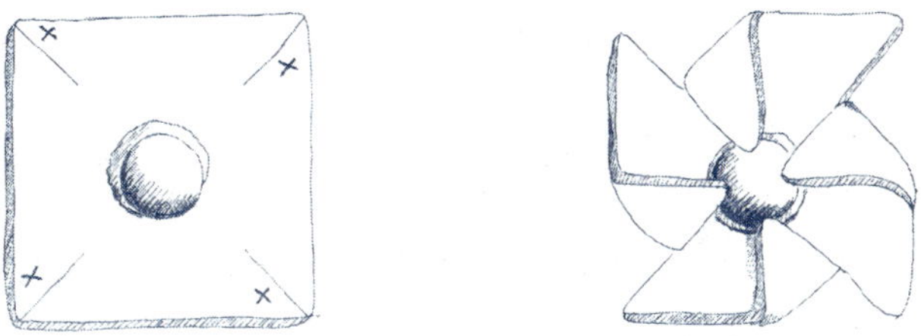

9 Top the remaining 10cm (4 inch) squares with a spoonful of apple purée and bring in two of the opposite corners to make a parcel (see below). Place on a greased baking tray.

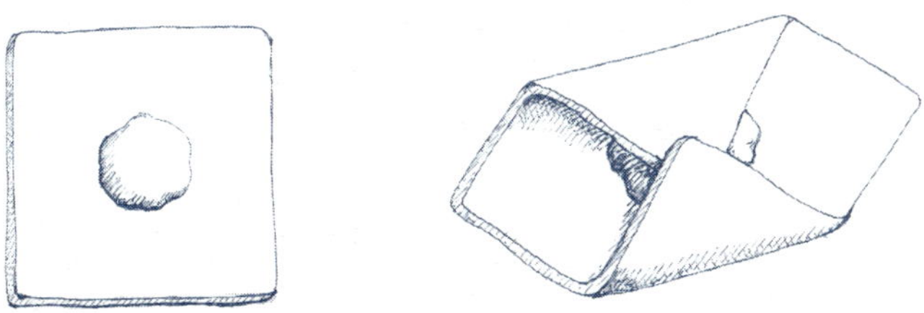

10 Leave the shapes to prove in a warm place for 20 minutes. This means that by the time you have shaped the final dough, the whirls should be ready to cook. Bake at 220°C/425°F/Gas Mark 7 for 15 minutes, until risen and starting to colour.

11 As soon as they come out of the oven, brush the pastries with the sieved apricot jam and decorate with flaked almonds and glacé cherries if wished. Transfer the pastries to wire racks to finish cooling.

The above fillings and decorations are only suggestions. Jam, pastry cream and fruit pie fillings all make excellent fillings and you can ice the finished pastries if you wish.

QUICK CHOCOLATE FUDGE

Americans make splendid fudge. You can sometimes see amazing displays of fudge making in shopping malls. The hot caramel mixture is worked, very entertainingly, on huge marble slabs with long paddles, until the mixture takes on the typical grainy fudge-like texture. Making fudge in the traditional way, by lengthy boiling and tedious beating is hard work. This recipe takes the time and effort out of the business.

MAKES: 700G (11/2LB)
PREPARATION TIME: 10 MINUTES + SETTING TIME

1 large can 400g (14oz) condensed milk
450g (1lb) plain chocolate
5ml (1tspn) vanilla extract

1 Melt the chocolate in a bowl over hot water or in the microwave.

2 Add the condensed milk and vanilla extract and mix well. You will find that this makes the chocolate go rather thick and grainy – fudge-like, in fact!

3 Turn the mixture into a lightly buttered 22.5cm (9 inch) square shallow tin, level the top and leave in a cool place to set.

4 Cut into squares and store in a cool place.

The fudge can be flavoured in a number of ways:

Add chopped walnuts or flaked almonds.

Add chopped glacé cherries or chopped dried apricots.

Soak a handful of raisins in a little rum. Leave until the raisins soak up the rum, then add to the fudge mix.

Chop a small bar of chocolate into little chunks. Lightly fold into the chocolate mixture.

Add mini marshmallows and chopped pecan nuts to the chocolate mixture to make rocky road fudge.

ANGEL CAKE

This classic American treat is probably the lightest of all cakes. Some say it is so delicate that it should not be cut but torn apart. Alternatively, choose a knife with a serrated blade and cut with a sawing action to prevent crushing the sponge. There are special angel cake tins, but you can use a savarin or deep ring mould or even sit a small round tin inside a larger one. It is the ring shape that you need.

SERVES: 8
PREPARATION TIME: 55 MINUTES + COOLING TIME

150g (5oz) caster sugar
90g (3½ oz) plain flour
2.5ml (½ tspn) salt
6 egg whites
5ml (1tspn) cream of tartar
Few drops each of almond and vanilla extract
5ml (1tspn) lemon juice

1 Grease a 2 litre (4pt) ring mould (see above) with oil and dust lightly with flour.

2 Mix half the sugar with the flour and salt and sift this mixture at least three times. This is essential to get air into the cake and give as much lightness as possible.

3 Using an electric whisk, beat the egg whites until foaming. Add the cream of tartar and continue whisking until the egg whites are very stiff. Gradually whisk in the remaining sugar, beating well between each addition. Whisk in the almond and vanilla extracts and the lemon juice.

4 Gradually fold the flour into the egg whites with a metal spoon, keeping the movements as light as possible.

5 Spoon the mixture into the prepared tin and bake at 180°C/350°F/Gas Mark 4 for 35–40 minutes, until springy to a light touch and well risen. Invert the tin on to a cooling rack, but do not remove. When cold, run a palette knife around the inner and outer rings and carefully remove the cake.

CHOCOLATE LAYER CAKE

SERVES: 10
PREPARATION TIME: 50 MINUTES + COOLING TIME

CAKE
175g (6oz) butter, softened
175g (6oz) light soft brown sugar
3 eggs, beaten
40g (1½ oz) cocoa powder
5ml (1tspn) baking powder

CHOCOLATE FUDGE ICING
225g (8oz) plain chocolate
75g (3oz) butter
2 eggs, beaten
About 275g (10oz) icing sugar, sifted

AMERICAN FROSTING
175g (6oz) caster sugar
1 egg white
30ml (2tbspn) hot water
Pinch of cream of tartar

American chocolate layer cakes can either have a rich chocolate icing or a crisp white frosting. Either way they are delicious.

1 To make the cake, cream together the butter and soft brown sugar until light and fluffy. Gradually beat in the eggs. Sift together the flour, cocoa powder and baking powder and carefully fold into the cake mixture.

2 Grease two 20cm (8 inch) round sandwich tins and line their bases with baking parchment. Divide the mixture evenly between the tins, levelling the tops. Bake at 190°C/375°F/Gas Mark 5 for 25–30 minutes until just firm to the touch. Turn out of the tins and cool on wire racks. When cold, split each cake in half through the centre and fill and top with either of the frostings.

To make the chocolate fudge icing:

1 Melt the chocolate and butter together in a bowl over a saucepan of hot water or in the microwave.

2 Stir in the egg and then beat in the icing sugar to make a thick icing.

3 Now beat until the mixture thickens and quickly use to fill and top the cakes. Swirl the top with a fork to make an attractive pattern. Leave in a cool place to set.

To make the American frosting:

1 Place all the ingredients in a heat-proof bowl over a saucepan of barely simmering water. Whisk until the mixture thickens and stands in soft peaks.

2 Remove from the heat and continue whisking until the mixture is cold.

3 Quickly use the frosting to fill and top the cakes, using a palette knife to lift the top into small peaks. Leave to set.

BLUEBERRY CINNAMON CAKE

SERVES: 6–8
PREPARATION TIME: 45 MINUTES

175g (6oz) self-raising flour
10ml (2tspn) ground cinnamon
50g (2oz) caster sugar
2 egg yolks
45ml (3tbspn) milk
50g (2oz) butter, melted and cooled slightly
175g (6oz) blueberries

TOPPING

25g (1oz) soft brown sugar
40g (1½ oz) plain flour
25g (1oz) butter
25g (1oz) walnuts, chopped
5ml (1tspn) ground cinnamon

1 Sift the flour, cinnamon and caster sugar into a bowl. Stir in the egg yolks, milk and melted butter and beat together until smooth.

2 Grease a 22.5cm (9 inch) round cake tin and line the bottom with baking parchment. Spread the mixture into the tin and level the top. Scatter the blueberries over.

3 To make the crumb topping, mix the sugar and flour and rub in the butter until the mixture resembles coarse breadcrumbs. Stir in the walnuts and cinnamon and sprinkle evenly over the fruit.

4 Bake in an oven preheated to 180°C/350°F/Gas Mark 4 for 30 minutes. Serve warm with ice cream or cold with coffee.

CHOCOLATE PEANUT BROWNIES

MAKES: 32
PREPARATION TIME: 40 MINUTES

200g (7oz) plain chocolate
110g (4oz) butter
175g (6oz) soft brown sugar
5 eggs
45ml (3tbspn) crunchy peanut butter
5ml (1tspn) vanilla extract
175g (6oz) plain flour

1 Melt the chocolate in a bowl over hot water or in the microwave.

2 Beat together the butter and sugar until light and fluffy. Gradually beat in the eggs, peanut butter and vanilla extract.

3 Stir in the chocolate and then fold in the flour. Don't worry that the mixture looks rather sloppy at this stage.

4 Grease a 33cm x 22.5cm (13 x 9 inch) Swiss roll tin. Pour the mixture into the tin and bake at 180°C/350°F/Gas Mark 4 for about 25 minutes. As with all brownies, these are better slightly undercooked. You may have to make this recipe several times to achieve the perfect level of gooeyness – but this is no hardship!

Try serving these brownies warm from the oven with a dollop of vanilla ice cream as a delicious dessert.

CORNBREAD

An American staple and the basis of Thanksgiving cornbread stuffing, this recipe is also excellent with chilli or casseroles. The ingredients below make quite a generous quantity. You might prefer to halve the ingredients, adding just the egg yolk, and bake for about 15–20 minutes, in a 16cm (6$^{1}/_{2}$ inch) square tin.

SERVES: 8
PREPARATION TIME: 30 MINUTES

175g (6oz) cornmeal
175g (6oz) plain flour
15ml (1tbspn) caster sugar
10ml (2tspn) baking powder
5ml (1tspn) salt
50g (2oz) butter, melted and cooled
1 egg, beaten
About 275ml ($^{1}/_{2}$pt) milk

1 Grease a 22.5cm (9 inch) square cake tin and line the base with baking parchment.

2 Sift together the cornmeal, flour, sugar, baking powder and salt in a large bowl.

3 Add the butter and egg and enough milk to just moisten the dry ingredients. Turn into the prepared tin.

4 Bake in an oven preheated to 220°C/425°F/Gas Mark 7 for 20–25 minutes, until the centre springs back when lightly pressed.

5 Cool in the tin for 15 minutes, then turn out carefully and complete cooling on a wire rack.

MUFFINS

American muffins are nothing like their English namesakes. They are more like large buns and are eaten at all times of the day, even for breakfast. Muffins may be sweet or savoury and are baked in special paper cases in deep bun tins. The tins come in standard and mini sizes. The following are basic sweet and savoury recipes, with a number of variations, but feel free to invent your own, too.

Sweet Muffins

MAKES: 6–8 STANDARD OR 20–24 MINI MUFFINS
PREPARATION TIME: 30–40 MINUTES

150g (5oz) plain flour
2.5ml (½tspn) baking powder 1tspn
50g (2oz) caster sugar
150ml (¼pt) full cream milk
50g (2oz) butter, melted and slightly cooled
1 egg, beaten
2.5ml (½tspn) vanilla extract

1 Sift the flour and baking powder into a bowl and stir in the sugar.

2 In a small bowl, blend together the milk, melted butter, egg and vanilla extract.

3 Pour the wet ingredients on to the dry ones and very quickly, using a large metal spoon, fold the two together. You are not trying to get a smooth mixture, merely to moisten the dry ingredients. Time is of the essence. The mix may look lumpy and curdled, but don't worry. This will ensure that the muffins are light.

4 At this point, you should quickly fold in your choice of flavouring.

5 Now spoon the mixture into muffin cases supported in muffin tins. Use bun cases in bun tins if you do not have the real things. The muffins will be squatter but taste just as good. Fill the cases almost to the top to result in the traditionally well risen muffin.

6 Bake the muffins in an oven preheated to 200°C/400°F/Gas Mark 6 for about 15–20 minutes for the mini ones and 30 minutes for the bigger variety. The muffins should look well risen and brown.

Savoury Muffins

MAKES: 6–8 STANDARD OR 20–24 MINI MUFFINS
PREPARATION TIME: 30–40 MINUTES

150g (6oz) plain flour
2.5ml (1/2 tspn) baking powder
5ml (1tspn) salt
2.5ml (1/2 tspn) mustard powder
Generous pinch of pepper
1 egg, beaten
150ml (1/4pt) milk
50g (2oz) butter, melted and slightly cooled

1 Sift the flour, salt, mustard powder and pepper into a large bowl.

2 Mix the egg, milk and butter in a small bowl.

3 Mix the dry and wet ingredients as in the previous recipe.

4 Add flavourings.

5 Pour the mixture into cases in tins and bake as for sweet muffins.

Blueberry Muffins

110g (4oz) blueberries
50g (2oz) hazelnuts, finely chopped
1 quantity sweet muffin mix

Add the blueberries and nuts at stage 4. Proceed as stated in the recipe.

Apple and Cinnamon Muffins

5ml (1tspn) ground cinnamon
1 large cooking apple, peeled, cored and finely chopped
Demerara sugar
1 quantity sweet muffin mix

Sift the cinnamon with the flour. Add the apple at stage 4. Sprinkle the muffins with demerara sugar prior to baking.

Wholemeal Banana Muffins

2 large bananas, mashed
Wholemeal flour
1 quantity sweet muffin mix

Replace half the plain flour with wholemeal flour and add the mashed bananas as stage 4. Proceed as stated in the recipe.

Double Chocolate Muffins

75g (3oz) chocolate chips (plain, milk, white or a mixture)
15ml ~~(1tbspn)~~ cocoa powder 2 tbspn
Chocolate buttons
1 quantity sweet muffin mix

Sift the cocoa powder with the flour mix. Stir in the chocolate chips at stage 4. Proceed with the recipe and, as soon as the muffins come out of the oven, top with two chocolate buttons – one milk chocolate and one white chocolate looks attractive. The buttons will melt but set again as the muffins cool.

Bacon and Corn Muffins

4 rashers streaky bacon, grilled until crisp, cooled and chopped
50g (2oz) canned sweetcorn kernels, drained
1 quantity savoury muffin mix

Add bacon and sweetcorn at stage 4. Proceed as stated in the recipe.

Cheese Muffins

110g (4oz) mature cheddar cheese, grated
15ml (1tbspn) chives, chopped

Add the chives and 90g (3½oz) of the cheese at stage 4. Sprinkle the remaining cheese on the muffins prior to baking.

COOK'S TIP

Muffins can be varied in many ways. The blueberries and apple can be swapped for any other fruit, such as raspberries, apricots, fresh or dried, and canned crushed pineapple, drained. Grated orange or lemon zest also adds flavour.

Savoury muffins can be flavoured with pesto, chopped olives, chopped onions and garlic. Grated carrot, crumbled blue cheese, chopped walnuts and sautéed mushrooms also make tasty alternatives. Why not experiment with combinations of these?

Muffins keep well for 2 or 3 days in an airtight tin and can be frozen very successfully but are best warm from the oven.

CINNAMON PECAN ROLLS

MAKES: 10
PREPARATION TIME: 1 HOUR 20 MINUTES + PROVING TIME

20g (3/4oz) fresh yeast or 15g (1/2oz) dried yeast
5ml (1tspn) caster sugar
90ml (6tbspn) warm water
450g (1lb) strong plain flour
5ml (1tspn) salt
50g (2oz) butter
1 egg, beaten
150ml (1/4pt) full cream milk, warmed
10ml (2tspn) ground cinnamon
30ml (2tbspn) soft brown sugar
50g (2oz) pecan nuts, chopped quite finely

1 Mix the yeast, sugar and warm water together and leave in a warm place until a froth forms.

2 Sift the flour and salt into a large bowl and rub in the butter until the mixture resembles fine breadcrumbs. Make a well in the centre and add the egg, yeast mixture and milk. Using first a wooden spoon and then your hands, work the flour into the liquid to form a rough dough.

3 Turn the dough on to a floured work surface and knead until it is smooth and elastic. Return the dough to a lightly floured bowl, cover with a clean tea towel and leave in a warm place until doubled in size – about 1½ hours.

4 Return the dough to a floured work surface and knock back to its original size. Roll the dough to a rectangle about 25 x 35cm (10 x 14 inches).

5 Mix the brown sugar and cinnamon together and sprinkle over the dough. Cover with the chopped pecans. Now roll up the dough like a Swiss roll, from the long side, and cut into 10 slices.

6 Arrange the swirls flat on a greased 22.5cm (9 inch) solid based round cake tin, with 7 rolls around the edge and 3 in the centre. Leave in a warm place for 30–45minutes. As the dough rises again, the swirls will join together.

7 Bake in an oven preheated to 190°C/375°F/Gas Mark 5 for 35–40 minutes. Remove from the tin, cool on a wire rack or eat warm.

CHOCOLATE CHIP COOKIES

Chocolate chip cookies are an American institution and they are found in many variations. They may be crisp or chewy, made with plain chocolate or with milk or even white chocolate. Some even use all three and add cocoa powder to the dough mix for the most decadent chocolate chip cookie of them all!

MAKES: ABOUT 50 BISCUITS
PREPARATION TIME: 30 MINUTES

110g (4oz) butter
110g (4oz) soft brown sugar
1 egg, beaten
2.5ml (1/2 tspn) vanilla extract
110g (4oz) plain flour
2.5ml (1/2 tspn) bicarbonate of soda
110g (4oz) good quality chocolate, chopped into small pieces

1 Cream the butter and sugar together until light and fluffy. Gradually beat in the egg and vanilla extract.

2 Sift the flour and bicarbonate of soda together and fold into the butter mixture. Stir in the chocolate chips.

3 Drop small spoonsful of the mixture on to greased baking trays, allowing plenty of room for the cookies to spread.

4 Bake at 180°C/350°F/Gas Mark 4 for 10–12 minutes, until lightly browned. Transfer to cooling racks, where they will crisp up as they cool. Store in an airtight tin.

CRANBERRY LOAF

SERVES: 10
PREPARATION TIME: 1 HOUR 30 MINUTES + COOLING TIME

225g (8oz) plain flour
7.5ml ($1^1/_2$ tspn) baking powder
2.5ml ($^1/_2$ tspn) bicarbonate of soda
50g (2oz) margarine
150g (5oz) cranberries, roughly chopped
Pinch of salt
75g (3oz) walnuts, chopped
175g (6oz) soft brown sugar
2 oranges, grated rind and juice
1 egg

1 Grease and line a 900g (2lb) loaf tin.

2 Sieve together the flour, baking powder and bicarbonate of soda into a large bowl, and rub in the margarine until the mixture resembles fine breadcrumbs. Stir in the cranberries, salt, nuts and sugar.

3 Whisk together the orange rind and juice and the egg and mix into the dry ingredients.

4 Turn the mixture into the prepared tin and bake at 180°C/350°F/Gas Mark 4 for about 1 hour 15 minutes, until a skewer inserted into the loaf comes out clean.

5 Allow the loaf to cool in the tin for 5 minutes, then turn out and finish cooling on a wire rack.

6 Store in an airtight tin for at least 24 hours before serving, sliced and buttered.

MARSHMALLOW CRISPIES

Marshmallows are a very popular cooking ingredient in America. You will only have to make this recipe once to ensure them a place in your store cupboard too.

MAKES: ABOUT 16
PREPARATION TIME: 10 MINUTES

50g (2oz) caster sugar
50g (2oz) butter
175g (6oz) golden syrup
75g (3oz) marshmallows
110g (4oz) crispy puffed rice cereal

1 Put the sugar, butter and syrup in a small pan over a low heat and stir until the sugar has dissolved and the butter is melted. Mix in the marshmallows and stir until melted.

2 Place the puffed rice in a bowl and slowly pour on the marshmallow mixture, stirring well until evenly coated.

3 Drop spoonsful of the mixture into bun cases and leave in a cool place to set.

CARROT CAKE

SERVES: 8
PREPARATION TIME: 45 MINUTES + COOLING TIME

225g (8oz) butter
225g (8oz) soft brown sugar
4 eggs, beaten
Grated rind 1 orange
15ml (1tbspn) lemon juice
225g (8oz) self-raising flour
5ml (1tspn) baking powder
110g (4oz) walnuts, chopped
350g (12oz) carrots, peeled and grated
225g (8oz) cream cheese
15ml (1tbspn) runny honey
110g (4oz) icing sugar

1 Grease two 20cm (8 inch) round sandwich tins and line the bases with baking parchment.

2 Beat together the butter and sugar and gradually beat in the eggs, orange rind and lemon juice.

3 Sieve together the flour and baking powder and fold it into the egg mixture. Stir in the walnuts and carrots until well blended.

4 Divide the mixture between the two tins, level the tops and bake at 180°C/350°F/Gas Mark 4 for 30–35 minutes, until well risen and firm to a light touch. Cool in the tins for 5 minutes, then turn out and finish cooling on wire racks.

5 Beat together the cream cheese, honey and icing sugar and use half to sandwich the cakes together. Spread the remainder over the top of the cake and mark into a pattern with a fork.

SPICY SOURED CREAM COOKIES

MAKES: 30 COOKIES
PREPARATION TIME: 20 MINUTES + COOLING TIME

150ml (1/4pt) vegetable oil
175g (6oz) soft brown sugar
2 eggs, beaten
225g (8oz) plain flour
5ml (1tspn) ground cinnamon
5ml (1tspn) ground mixed spice
5ml (1tspn) bicarbonate of soda
Pinch of salt
150ml (1/4pt) soured cream

1 Place the oil and sugar in a bowl and mix well. Add the eggs and beat until thoroughly mixed.

2 Sift together the flour, cinnamon, mixed spice, bicarbonate of soda and salt and add in spoonsful to the egg mix alternately with the soured cream, until all the ingredients are incorporated. Mix well.

3 Drop small spoonsful of the mixture on lightly greased baking trays, allowing room for the cookies to spread.

4 Bake at 190°C/375°F/Gas Mark 5 for about 10 minutes. The biscuits will be soft, so leave on the trays until they start to firm up and then transfer to wire racks to finish cooling.

5 These cookies will store well in an airtight container. They have an unusual, chewy texture and a spicy flavour that makes them particularly suitable at Christmas.

OATMEAL CAKE

SERVES: 8
PREPARATION TIME: 55 MINUTES + COOLING TIME

CAKE
275ml (1/2pt) boiling water
175g (6oz) rolled oats
110g (4oz) butter
275g (10oz) soft brown sugar
2 eggs, beaten
5ml (1tspn) vanilla extract
175g (6oz) plain flour
5ml (1tspn) baking powder
5ml (1tspn) ground cinnamon
Pinch of salt

TOPPING
75g (3oz) butter
75g (3oz) soft brown sugar
15ml (1tbspn) golden syrup
50g (2oz) dessicated coconut
75g (30z) walnuts, chopped
50g (2oz) rolled oats

1 First make the cake. Pour the boiling water over the oats, stir to mix and then leave to cool.

2 Beat the butter and sugar together until light and fluffy. Beat in the eggs and the vanilla extract.

3 Sift together the flour, baking powder, cinnamon and salt and fold into the butter mixture with the cooled oats.

4 Turn the mixture into a greased and lined 22.5cm (9 inch) round cake tin and bake at 180°C/350°F/Gas Mark 4 for 30–35 minutes, until risen and golden brown. Turn out on to a rack to cool.

5 To make the topping, place the butter, sugar and golden syrup in a pan over a medium heat until the butter has melted. Take the pan off the heat and stir in the nuts and oats. Spoon this mixture over the top of the cooled cake and flash under a hot grill until bubbling and golden brown. Watch carefully as the mixture can burn quite easily. Allow to cool before serving.

DRINKS

RECIPES

1

PINA COLADA

A Texan/Mexican special, combining the flavours of pineapple and coconut with rum.

2

MANHATTAN

Probably the most famous of all American cocktails.

3

MINT JULEP

A drink that conjures up images of Southern belles or the excitement of the Kentucky Derby.

4

HARVEY WALLBANGER

Harvey was a Californian surfer but where the Wallbanger comes from is open to question!

5

HOT BUTTERED RUM

A warming drink, which will certainly put a tingle into chilly fingers and toes.

6

WHISKY SOUR

There are many variations on this drink, but whisky sour made with bourbon is the original.

7

CHOCOLATE MILKSHAKE

As if there were not enough chocolate recipes in this book, this one ensures that you can drink it as well!

8

STRAWBERRY MILKSHAKE

A thick, fruity and delicious drink for summer days.

9

ICED TEA

A remarkably refreshing drink for a hot summer's day.

Although other countries may dispute it, America can probably justifiably lay claim to inventing the cocktail. The earliest references describe a cocktail as "a stimulating liquor, composed of spirits of any kind, sugar, water and bitters". However, it really came into its own during the prohibition years of the 1920s and 1930s, when mixing it with other flavours was the only way to make bootleg alcohol palatable. Talullah Bankhead, the film star, probably did as much as anyone to popularise the cocktail. Such was her fame that her actions were slavishly copied, and before long her fans were drinking cocktails all over America.

Cocktail recipes are very accurately written with precise instructions as to their manufacture. Some specific equipment is desirable but a large, screw-topped jar will make a perfectly acceptable cocktail shaker – it just doesn't look quite glamorous enough for Talullah! A long-handled spoon is needed for stirring and an ice bucket is useful to store the quantities of ice cubes and crushed ice you will require. A small measure is also useful. A lot of cocktail recipes are written as proportions – 1 part of this and 2 parts of that – so a constant measure helps.

Most cocktails call for a blend of spirits, mixers and flavourings. Keeping the fixings for any imaginable cocktail would be prohibitively expensive. It is worth remembering that it is possible to buy miniatures of most spirits and this is particularly useful for the more unusual cocktail ingredients. However, if you are planning to make cocktails regularly, then it is worth investing in bottles of good whisky and gin.

Part of the attraction of cocktails is the decoration. Little parasols and plastic monkeys can be taking the thing a little far, but slices of fresh fruit, twists of citrus peel and fresh flowers can all add to the appeal, as can frosted glasses.

HARVEY WALLBANGER

MAKES: 2 GLASSES
PREPARATION TIME: 5 MINUTES

120ml (4 fl oz) vodka
225ml (8 fl oz) fresh orange juice
30ml (2tbspn) Galliano liqueur

1 Pour the vodka and orange juice into a cocktail shaker or chilled large screw-topped jar, add ice and shake well.

2 Strain the mixture into squat tumblers, half filled with ice.

3 Carefully pour the Galliano over the back of a spoon held close to the top of the cocktail, so that it floats on the surface.

HOT BUTTERED RUM

MAKES: 2 MUGS
PREPARATION TIME: 5 MINUTES

120ml (4 fl oz) white or dark rum
2 sticks cinnamon, about 10cm (4 inches) long
6 whole cloves
10ml (2tspn) caster sugar
Boiling water
Butter

1 Pour the rum into 2 mugs and add the cloves and sugar. Fill up the mugs with boiling water and float a knob of butter on the top.

2 Serve the drink piping hot, sipped through the melted butter, with the cinnamon sticks as stirrers.

WHISKY SOUR

MAKES: **2 GLASSES**
PREPARATION TIME: **10 MINUTES**

120ml (4 fl oz) bourbon
30ml (2tbspn) lemon juice
15ml (1tbspn) icing sugar
Egg white, beaten
Caster sugar

1 Frost 2 white wine glasses by dipping the rims first in egg white and then in caster sugar. Chill.

2 Mix together icing sugar and lemon juice until the sugar has dissolved. Pour into a shaker with the bourbon and some crushed ice, and shake well.

3 Strain into the glasses and decorate with a twist of lemon zest.

CHOCOLATE MILKSHAKE

MAKES: **2 GLASSES**
PREPARATION TIME: **5 MINUTES**

15ml (1tbspn) drinking chocolate
Boiling water
425ml (3/4pt) full cream milk, chilled
30ml (2tbspn) vanilla ice cream
2 chocolate flakes

1 Dissolve the chocolate powder with a little boiling water and then blend with the milk.

2 Place the chocolate milk in a liquidiser with the ice cream and blend until just smooth.

3 Pour the drinks into chilled glasses and add a chocolate flake to each. Serve at once.

STRAWBERRY MILKSHAKE

MAKES: 2 GLASSES
PREPARATION TIME: 5 MINUTES

275ml ($\frac{1}{2}$pt) full cream milk, chilled
150g (5oz) strawberry yoghurt
110g (4oz) fresh ripe strawberries
30ml (2tbspn) vanilla ice cream

1 Place the milk, yoghurt and all but two of the strawberries in a liquidiser and blend until smooth.

2 Pour into 2 tall glasses and top each one with a spoonful of ice cream. Decorate with the reserved strawberries and serve at once.

ICED TEA

SERVES: 6
PREPARATION TIME: 30 MINUTES + COOLING TIME

6 tea bags (choose a type with a good flavour)
30ml (2tbspn) caster sugar
Several sprigs of mint
275ml (1/2pt) freshly squeezed orange juice
Juice of 1 lime or half a lemon
1 small orange, sliced
1 lemon, sliced

1 Make up the tea using the tea bags and about 1.2 litres (2pts) of boiling water. Allow to infuse for about 20 minutes. It will look quite strong, but remember that it will be diluted later.

2 Remove the tea bags and stir in the sugar and about 4 or 5 sprigs of mint. Leave until quite cold.

3 Remove the mint. Pack a large glass jug with lots of ice. Pour in the tea, followed by the orange and lemon or lime juice and 4 or 5 fresh sprigs of mint.

4 Add the orange and lemon slices and stir thoroughly.

5 Serve in tall glasses with more ice.

This drink is something like a non-alcoholic Pimms. It is therefore ideal to serve at a summer party, to drivers and non-drivers alike.

Celebration and Holiday Menus

Americans certainly know how to enjoy themselves during holidays and weekends, and, since American workers normally have only two weeks' annual holiday, they make the most of evenings, weekends and public holidays too. The latter include commemorations of George Washington and Martin Luther King. As the right of Americans to follow the faith of their choice is upheld in the Constitution, Christian festivals are not such important national holidays as in Europe. In fact, Christmas is often just a one-day break, but occasions such as Thanksgiving are celebrated nationwide.

The Fourth of July celebration provides the ideal occasion for a picnic with family and friends. July the fourth is Independence Day, commemorating the 1776 Declaration of Independence following the hard-fought war between England and her then American colony. Towns and villages throughout the country celebrate with fireworks, parades and picnics.

Hallowe'en, the 31st of October, marks the start of the American holiday season, which includes Thanksgiving and Christmas and ends with New Year celebrations. Children dress up as spooks and ghouls and "trick-or-treat" their neighbourhoods. Most houses are decorated with Jack-O-Lanterns, and supermarkets have piles of huge orange pumpkins stacked outside their doors.

The Pilgrim Fathers, who crossed the sea from England to the "New World" in the seventeenth century, quickly discovered that the seeds and plants they had brought with them did not flourish in the harsh weather conditions of New England. If they had not had the help of native Americans, who introduced them to the local plants and offered shelter, the Fathers would have perished. After their first successful harvest, they celebrated with a feast of Thanksgiving, and it was to the native Americans as well as to God that they gave their thanks – a fact which seemed to be forgotten in later years. Thanksgiving is celebrated on the last Thursday of November and usually includes a traditional meal of roast turkey, cornbread stuffing and cranberry relish.

Brunch is an institution in America. On Sunday mornings, hotels and restaurants lay out huge brunch buffets. Platters of scrambled eggs, crispy bacon, sizzling sausages and hash browns are kept warm, while a chef cooks fresh waffles, pancakes and omelettes and fills bowls with fresh fruit, whipped cream and maple syrup. To fill any spaces, there are baskets of muffins and Danish pastries, with cereals and porridge for the brave or foolish! Brunch starts at about 10am and continues for several hours. Needless to say, after this Sunday lunch is not a major event.

On the following pages, you will find suggestions for menus to accompany some of these occasions.

SUMMER BARBECUE MENU

Barbecue Ribs *(see page 114)*

Hamburgers *(see page 43)*

Biscuits

Corn Relish

Barbecued Baked Beans

Twice-Baked Potatoes *(see page 131)*

Fruit Kebabs

Butterscotch Sundaes

Iced Tea *(see page 214)*

BISCUITS

American biscuits are rather like savoury scones. They are often served in restaurants, as we might be offered bread rolls, before a meal. Since they are usually served warm, with lashings of butter and in copious quantities, there is a serious danger that you will be full of biscuits before you actually reach your main course.

MAKES: ABOUT 10
PREPARATION TIME: 30 MINUTES

225g (8oz) plain flour
12.5ml (2½ tspn) baking powder
5ml (1tspn) salt
60g (2½ oz) butter
2.5ml (½ tspn) dried thyme
5ml (1tspn) fresh parsley, chopped
180ml (6fl oz) whipping cream

1 Sift the flour, baking powder and salt into a large bowl. Cut the butter into cubes and rub into the flour until the mixture resembles fine breadcrumbs. Stir in the herbs.

2 Stir the cream into the flour mixture to give a soft dough. Knead very lightly on a floured work surface and roll out to 1cm (½ inch) thick. Cut out 6cm (2½ inch) rounds, rolling out the trimmings again as necessary.

3 Place the biscuits on baking trays and cook in an oven preheated to 220°C/425°F/Gas Mark 7 for about 15 minutes, until golden brown. Serve warm.

BARBECUED BAKED BEANS

SERVES: 6
PREPARATION TIME: 20 MINUTES

25g (1oz) butter
1 large onion, chopped
6 rashers rindless streaky bacon, chopped
2.5ml (1/2 tspn) chilli powder, or to taste
200g (7oz) can chopped tomatoes in juice
435g (15 1/2 oz) can baked beans
Salt and pepper
15ml (1tbspn) Worcestershire sauce

1 Melt the butter in a saucepan over a medium heat. Add the onion and fry gently for 5 minutes. Add the bacon to the pan and cook for a further 10 minutes.

2 Stir in the chilli powder and cook for 2 minutes, then add the tomatoes and baked beans.

3 Stir well and simmer gently until heated through. Add salt and pepper to taste and the Worcestershire sauce. Serve piping hot.

CORN RELISH

MAKES: 900G (2LB)
PREPARATION TIME: 30 MINUTES

75g (3oz) soft brown sugar
5ml (1tspn) mustard powder
5ml (1tspn) salt
570ml (1pt) white wine vinegar
450g (1lb) frozen sweetcorn kernels
1 green pepper, deseeded and finely chopped
1 red pepper, deseeded and finely chopped
1 onion, finely chopped

1 In a small bowl, mix together the sugar, mustard powder and salt with enough of the vinegar to make a smooth paste. Pour the remaining vinegar into a large pan on a medium heat and whisk in the mustard mixture until evenly blended.

2 Add the sweetcorn, peppers and onion and simmer gently for about 20 minutes, until the vegetables are tender.

3 Pour the relish into clean, heated jars and seal while hot. Store, once cooled, in a cool, dark place.

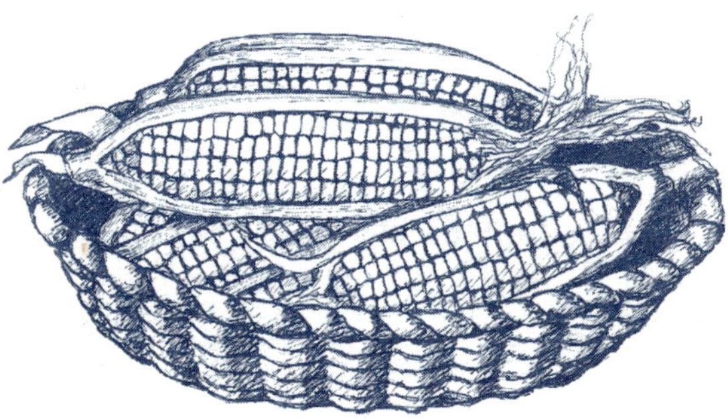

FRUIT KEBABS

MAKES: As many as you wish, adjust quantities accordingly
PREPARATION TIME: 50 minutes + standing time

1 small unsliced loaf, 2 days old
Butter
Soft brown sugar
Apples
Bananas
Lemon juice
Fresh pineapple
Rum (optional)

1 Trim the crusts off the bread and discard them. Cut the bread into cubes about 2cm (3/4 inch) square.

2 Melt about 110g (4oz) of butter for every 350g (12oz) of bread. Place the cubes of bread in a large bowl and slowly trickle in the melted butter, tossing the cubes as you do so, to evenly coat the bread. Allow to cool, stirring occasionally to ensure that the cubes stay separate. Sprinkle in about 75g (3oz) soft brown sugar for every 350g (12oz) of bread and mix thoroughly.

3 Meanwhile, quarter and core the apples and cut into bite-sized chunks. Sprinkle with lemon juice to prevent browning.

4 Peel the bananas, slice thickly and sprinkle with lemon juice.

5 Peel and trim the pineapple and cut it into bite-sized chunks.

6 In a bowl, layer the fruit, sprinkling each layer with sugar, until all the fruit is used. Sprinkle generously with rum, if using, and leave to stand for at least 1 hour. Stir well.

7 Thread the fruit and bread cubes on to small skewers. They don't have to be identical, but try to get a good distribution of flavours on each skewer. Grill for about 10 minutes, turning frequently. The bread will become crisp and caramelised.

BUTTERSCOTCH SUNDAES

SERVES: 4
PREPARATION TIME: 15 MINUTES

110g (4oz) golden syrup
110g (4oz) light soft brown sugar
25g (1oz) butter
30ml (2tbspn) hot water
60ml (4tbspn) double cream
2.5ml (½ tspn) vanilla extract
570ml (1pt) vanilla ice cream
50g (2oz) walnuts, chopped

1 First make the sauce. Put the syrup, sugar and butter in a saucepan over a low heat and stir until the sugar has dissolved and the butter and syrup have melted. Bring to the boil and simmer for 3 minutes.

2 Remove from the heat and carefully add the hot water. The mixture may sizzle a bit, so watch your hands.

3 Cool a little and then add the cream and vanilla extract.

4 Place scoops of ice cream in 4 sundae dishes, pour over the warm sauce and sprinkle with the chopped nuts. Serve at once.

FOURTH OF JULY PICNIC MENU

Fried Chicken With Mustard Dip

Tuna Cream

Tomatoes

Potato Salad (see page 127)

Coleslaw (see page 129)

French Bread

Peach Upside-Down Cake

Chocolate Chip Cookies (see page 198)

Lemonade

FRIED CHICKEN AND MUSTARD DIP

Make the fried chicken recipe on page 85. After cooking, drain the chicken thoroughly on crumpled kitchen paper and cool as quickly as possible. You will find, if you make the chicken on the morning of the picnic, that it will retain its crispness. Serve it with the tangy mustard dip below.

MUSTARD DIP

SERVES: 6–8
PREPARATION TIME: 10 MINUTES

2 egg yolks, at room temperature
15ml (1tbspn) made mustard
Salt and black pepper
5ml (1tspn) lemon juice
275ml (1/2pt) olive oil
15ml (1tbspn) boiling water
3–4 spring onions, finely chopped

1 Stir together the egg yolks, mustard, seasoning and lemon juice until well blended.

2 Very slowly add the oil, whisking all the time. As you begin to get a thick sauce, you will be able to add the oil more quickly, but keep whisking all the time.

3 Beat in the boiling water. I have found that if the sauce has a slight tendency to separate during whisking, the boiling water seems to pull it back together again.

4 Stir in the onions. Pack into a sealable container and chill.

TUNA CREAM

SERVES: 6
PREPARATION TIME: 15 MINUTES + CHILLING TIME

275g (10oz) cream cheese
450g (1lb) canned tuna, drained
4 spring onions, finely chopped
1 stalk of celery, finely chopped
4 gherkins, finely chopped
75g (3oz) walnuts, chopped
2.5ml (1/2 tspn) salt
Pinch of black pepper
Pinch of mustard powder
Pinch of mixed herbs

1 Soften the cream cheese in a bowl and add the flaked tuna. Mix together – lightly for a rough mixture or more thoroughly for a smoother cream.

2 Mix in the onions, celery, gherkins and walnuts, with the salt, pepper, mustard and herbs. Taste and adjust the seasonings if required.

3 Turn into a plastic tub and chill for at least 2 hours.

Tuna canned in brine will work well in this recipe, but the result is richer if made with the fish in oil.

PEACH UPSIDE-DOWN CAKE

SERVES: 6–8

PREPARATION TIME: 50 MINUTES + COOLING TIME

4 large, ripe peaches or a large can of peach halves in natural juice
50g (2oz) butter
50g (2oz) soft brown sugar
50g (2oz) blanched almonds, chopped
110g (4oz) margarine, softened
110g (4oz) caster sugar
Grated zest 1 orange
2 eggs
175g (6oz) self-raising flour
30ml (2tbspn) orange juice

1 If using fresh peaches, cut in half, remove the stones and place in a bowl. Cover with boiling water and drain after 2 minutes. The skins should slip off easily. If using canned peaches, simply drain them.

2 Melt the butter and sugar together in a small pan over a low heat and pour into a solid-based 20cm (8 inch) round cake tin. Arrange the peach halves, cut side up, over the butter mixture and sprinkle the chopped almonds in the gaps between the peaches.

3 Cream together the margarine and caster sugar with the orange zest until light and fluffy, then gradually beat in the eggs.

4 Fold in the flour and orange juice. Spread the mixture carefully over the whole base without disturbing the fruit.

5 Bake at 190°C/375°F/Gas Mark 5 for about 30–35 minutes, until well risen and firm to a gentle touch.

6 Cool the cake in the tin for 10 minutes, then turn out and finish cooling on a wire rack. Cut into slices.

LEMONADE

Homemade lemonade thankfully bears little resemblance to the shop-bought variety. It is tangy and refreshing. Dilute it with water to serve, or with soda or tonic water if you prefer a fizzy drink.

MAKES: A LOT! IT WILL STORE IN THE REFRIGERATOR FOR WEEKS
PREPARATION TIME: 20 MINUTES + COOLING TIME

5 lemons
900g (2lb) granulated sugar
1litre ($1\frac{3}{4}$pt) water
25g (1oz) citric acid (see Cook's tip below)

1 Carefully grate the zest from the lemons, trying to avoid the white pith. Squeeze out the juice and reserve.

2 Place the sugar and water in a large pan with the lemon zest and stir over a low heat until the sugar has dissolved. Bring to the boil and simmer for 10 minutes.

3 Cool the liquid, then add the citric acid and lemon juice. Strain and store in bottles in the fridge. Dilute as required.

Citric acid should be obtainable from your local chemist. It is usually sold as a white powder.

CHOCOLATE FUDGE BROWNIES

MAKES: 16
PREPARATION TIME: 30 MINUTES + COOLING TIME

110g (4oz) butter
110g (4oz) plain chocolate, broken into squares
275g (10oz) light soft brown sugar
4 eggs, beaten
40g (1½ oz) cocoa powder
225g (8oz) self-raising flour
75g (3oz) pecans, chopped

1 Place the butter and chocolate in a saucepan over a low heat and stir gently until melted.

2 Stir in the sugar and beat in the eggs.

3 Sift together the flour and cocoa and add to the chocolate mixture. Mix very thoroughly and fold in the pecans.

4 Grease a 30 x 35cm (12 x 14 inch) Swiss roll tin and line the base with baking parchment. Pour in the brownie mixture and bake in an oven preheated to 180°C/350°F/Gas Mark 4 for about 15 minutes. It is essential that these brownies are slightly undercooked. Test with a skewer – this is one of the few occasions when you want some of the mixture to cling to it.

5 Cool in the tin, then cut into squares. Serve warm, with vanilla ice cream.

TOFFEE APPLES

A popular treat at Hallowe'en, young "trick-or-treaters" might expect to receive several of these sticky fruits. The homemade variety, rich and buttery, are vastly superior to shop-bought ones.

MAKES: 12
PREPARATION TIME: 30 MINUTES

12 eating apples
175g (6oz) golden syrup
350g (12oz) soft brown sugar
40g (1½oz) butter
150ml (¼pt) water
5ml (1tspn) vinegar

1 Wash the apples and dry them thoroughly. Remove the stalks and push a wooden skewer deep into each apple from the stalk end.

2 Put the syrup, sugar, butter, water and vinegar into a large, heavy based pan and stir over a gentle heat until the sugar has dissolved. Bring to the boil and bubble briskly until caramel coloured. A drop in cold water should quickly set and snap cleanly.

3 Dip each apple in the hot toffee and twist to coat completely. Quickly dip in cold water to set the coating and stand on greaseproof paper until cold and totally set. With the last few apples, you may have to pour the toffee over using a spoon, as the level of toffee in the pan will have gone down.

4 If not eaten immediately, or given as gifts, the apples should be wrapped in cellophane as the toffee quickly goes sticky if exposed to the atmosphere.

THANKSGIVING DINNER MENU

Roast Turkey With Maple Butter and Gravy

Cornbread Stuffing

Traditional Oyster Stuffing

Cranberry and Orange Sauce

Green Beans

Parsnip Gratin (see page 134)

Sweet Potatoes With Marshmallows

Pumpkin Pie With Whipped Cream

Coffee

Chocolate Fudge (see page 184)

ROAST TURKEY WITH MAPLE BUTTER AND GRAVY

SERVES: 8

PREPARATION TIME: 3 HOURS 30 MINUTES

150ml (1/4pt) dry cider
75ml (5tbspn) maple syrup
10ml (2tspn) lemon rind, grated
15ml (1tbspn) fresh thyme, chopped
15ml (1tbspn) fresh parsley, chopped
175g (6oz) butter, softened
14lb turkey, giblets removed
1 onion, roughly chopped
1 lemon
570ml (1pt) chicken or turkey stock
45ml (3tbspn) plain flour
Salt and pepper

1 Place the cider and maple syrup in a pan and boil for 10–15 minutes, until reduced by half. Cool. Stir in the lemon rind, thyme and parsley and beat this mixture into the butter. Chill.

2 Place the turkey in a large roasting pan. Lift up the skin covering the breast and smear the meat with half the butter mixture. Reposition the skin and dot with half the remaining butter.

3 Place the onion and lemon in the cavity of the turkey. Cover with foil and cook at 180°C/350°F/Gas Mark 4 for 3 hours, or until cooked. Test by piercing the thickest part of the leg with a sharp knife – the juices should run clear. Transfer to a serving dish, cover with fresh foil and leave to stand.

4 Meanwhile, drain the juices from the pan and add to the stock. Heat to near boiling. Mix the remaining butter with the flour in a small bowl. Whisk into the stock and bring to the boil, continuing to whisk. Add salt and pepper to taste.

5 Serve the turkey with the gravy and either or both of the stuffings below.

THANKSGIVING CORNBREAD STUFFING

SERVES: 8
PREPARATION TIME: 1 HOUR

225g (8oz) pork sausagemeat
110g (4oz) butter, melted
1 large onion, chopped
2 stalks of celery, chopped
1 small green pepper, deseeded and chopped
1 quantity of cornbread (see page 191)
25g (1oz) fresh parsley, chopped
5ml (1tspn) fresh sage, finely chopped
110g (4oz) walnuts, chopped
1 egg, beaten
Salt and black pepper
Turkey or chicken stock

1 Fry the sausagemeat in a large pan over a medium to high heat until browned, using a wooden spoon to break up the lumps. Transfer to a bowl.

2 Heat the butter in a pan over a medium heat. Add the onion and cook for 5 minutes. Add the celery and green pepper and cook for a further 5 minutes. Transfer to the bowl with the sausagemeat.

3 Crumble the cornbread roughly and add to the sausagemeat with the parsley, sage and walnuts. Mix in the beaten egg.

4 Add salt and pepper to taste and mix in enough stock to make a moist but not sloppy mix. Stir gently so that the cornbread does not totally break down.

5 You can stuff the turkey with this mixture, but I prefer to cook it separately, in a lightly greased, shallow oven-proof dish, which gives it a crispy top. Bake at 190°C/350°F/Gas Mark 5 for about 30 minutes.

TRADITIONAL OYSTER STUFFING

SERVES: 8
PREPARATION TIME: 1 HOUR 20 MINUTES

1 small white loaf, crusts removed, cut into 1cm (1/2 inch) cubes
225g (8oz) frozen chopped spinach, defrosted and drained
50g (2oz) butter
1 small onion, finely chopped
3 stalks of celery, finely chopped
3 cloves garlic, crushed
350g (12oz) fresh oysters or canned or bottled oysters, drained
30ml (2tbspn) fresh parsley, chopped
3 eggs, beaten
Salt and pepper
Chicken stock

1 Spread the bread cubes on baking sheets and cook in an oven preheated to 140°C/275°F/Gas mark 1 for 15 minutes, until dry but not coloured. Transfer to a large bowl and mix in the spinach.

2 Melt half the butter in a pan over a medium heat. Add the onion and cook for 5 minutes. Stir in the celery and garlic and cook for a further 5 minutes. Stir the vegetable mixture into the bread one.

3 Melt the remaining butter in a pan. Add the oysters and cook, stirring, for 2 minutes. Add to the bread with the parsley and eggs. Mix well and season to taste.

4 Add enough stock to make a moist but not sloppy mixture.

5 Transfer to a large, lightly greased baking tin and cover with foil. Bake in an oven preheated to 180°C/350°F/Gas Mark 4 for 30 minutes. Remove the foil and cook for a further 15–20 minutes, until the top is crispy.

CRANBERRY AND ORANGE SAUCE

MAKES: ABOUT 275ML (1/2PT)
PREPARATION TIME: 20 MINUTES

225g (8oz) fresh cranberries
150ml (1/4pt) port
110g (4oz) granulated sugar
Pinch of salt
45ml (3tbspn) orange juice
5ml (1tspn) cornflour
2.5ml (1/2tspn) mustard powder
5ml (1tspn) lemon juice
Pinch of ground cloves
50g (2oz) raisins
15ml (1tbspn) orange zest, grated
5ml (1tspn) lemon zest, grated

1 Place the cranberries and port in a heavy based saucepan over a medium heat. Cook for about 10 minutes, stirring occasionally, until the cranberries burst. Add the sugar and salt and stir until dissolved.

2 Mix together the orange juice, cornflour, mustard powder, lemon juice and cloves in a small bowl until smooth. Stir into the cranberry mixture.

3 Add the raisins and orange and lemon zests and simmer, stirring occasionally, for 5 minutes. Cool. This sauce may be stored in the refrigerator for up to 4 days. Serve at room temperature.

SWEET POTATOES WITH MARSHMALLOWS

SERVES: 8
PREPARATION TIME: 1 HOUR 30 MINUTES

1.8kg (4lb) sweet potatoes, peeled and cut into 2.5cm (1 inch) cubes
150g (5oz) soft brown sugar
75g (3oz) butter
Pinch of ground cinnamon
Pinch of ground nutmeg
5ml (1tspn) salt
110g (4oz) miniature marshmallows

1 Heat together the sugar, butter, cinnamon, nutmeg and salt in a small pan over a low heat, until the sugar dissolves.

2 Place the potatoes in a large baking dish and pour over the sugar mixture, tossing the potatoes until evenly coated. Cover the dish tightly with foil.

3 Bake at 190°C/375°F/Gas Mark 5 for 50 minutes. Remove the foil and cook, basting occasionally, for a further 20 minutes.

4 Increase the oven temperature to maximum. Sprinkle the marshmallows over the dish and return to the oven for 4–5 minutes, until the topping melts and starts to brown. Serve at once.

If you cannot find mini marshmallows in your supermarket (look in the baking section), use larger ones (white only), cut into pieces with scissors.

PUMPKIN PIE

SERVES: 8
PREPARATION TIME: 1 HOUR 10 MINUTES

PASTRY
175g (6oz) plain flour
25g (1oz) icing sugar
75g (3oz) butter
1 egg yolk
Cold water to bind

FILLING
400g (14oz) pumpkin purée (see Cook's tip below)
50g (2oz) butter, melted
150g (5oz) soft brown sugar
2.5ml (1/2 tspn) ground cinnamon
2.5ml (1/2 tspn) ground nutmeg
2.5ml (1/2 tspn) ground ginger
3 eggs, separated
150ml (1/4 pt) double cream

1 First make the pastry. Sift the flour and icing sugar into a bowl.

Add the butter and rub into the flour until the mixture resembles fine breadcrumbs. Mix in the egg and enough water to make a firm dough.

2 Roll out the pastry on a lightly floured work surface and use it to line a 22.5cm (9 inch) pie dish.

3 Place the pumpkin purée into a large bowl and beat in the melted butter, sugar and spices. Mix in the egg yolks and cream.

4 Whisk the egg whites until stiff and fold carefully into the pumpkin mixture. Pour into the pastry case.

5 Bake at 180°C/350°F/Gas Mark 4 for about 45 minutes, until firm to the touch. Cool and serve warm or cold with whipped cream.

The secret of a good pumpkin pie is to have the purée as dry as possible. For this reason, resort to canned pumpkin purée only if desperate. To achieve the best results, cut a small pumpkin in half and scoop out the seeds and strings. Place, cut side down, on a greased baking sheet and bake at 160°C/325°F/Gas Mark 3 for about 1 hour, until tender. Remove the pumpkin from the oven carefully as the baking tray may be awash with juices – discard these. Scoop the pulp out of the shell and liquidise or push through a sieve to give a smooth purée.

SUNDAY BRUNCH MENU

Waffles

Cornmeal Pancakes

Maple Syrup

Strawberries

Whipped Cream

Scrambled Eggs

Bacon

Grilled Tomatoes

Hash Browns *(see page 126)*

Fresh Fruit Platter

French Toast *(see page 51)*

Coffee

Useful Information

GLOSSARY

The expression that America and Britain are "two nations divided by a common language" certainly has some truth when it comes to food. The ingredients and cooking methods are rarely strange but the terms used can sometimes be confusing. If this book inspires you to try original American recipes, it may be useful to glance down the following lists.

AMERICAN TERM	BRITISH EQUIVALENT
Biscuits	Scones
Butter, sweet	Unsalted butter, whipped
Chips	Potato crisps
Chocolate, semi sweet	Plain chocolate
Chocolate, sweet	Milk chocolate
Club soda	Soda water
Cookie	Sweet biscuits
Cornstarch	Corflour
Corn syrup	Golden syrup
Crack	Biscuits for cheese
Filberts	Hazelnuts
Graham crackers	Digestive biscuits (more or less!)
Cream, light	Single cream

Cream, heavy	Double cream
Flapjacks	Pancakes
Flour, all purpose	Plain white flour
Flour, cake	Self-raising flour
Flour, wholewheat	Use half and half white and wholemeal
Fries	Chips
Jelly	Jam
Oatmeal	Rolled oats
Shrimps	Prawns
Shortening	White vegetable fat
Sugar, confectioner's	Icing sugar
Sugar, powdered	Caster sugar
Tomato paste	Tomato purée
Tomato sauce	Thin tomato purée not tomato ketchup

Vegetables

Beans, string	Runner beans
Beets	Beetroot
Corn	Sweetcorn or maize
Eggplant	Aubergine
Bell peppers	Sweet green peppers
Rutabaga	Swede
Scallions	Spring onions
Zucchini	Courgettes

Cooking terms

Broiler	Grill
Dressing	Stuffing
Sherbet	Sorbet

Index